Women in
African Literature Today
15

Women in
African Literature Today

A review
Editor: ELDRED DUROSIMI JONES
Associate Editor: EUSTACE PALMER
Editorial Assistant: MARJORIE JONES

JAMES CURREY
LONDON

AFRICA WORLD PRESS
TRENTON N.J.

Africa World Press, Inc.
P.O. Box 1892
Trenton, N.J. 08607

First American Edition 1987
©James Currey Ltd. 1987

Library of Congress Catalog Card Number: 87-70491

ISBN: 0-86543-056-X
        0-86543-057-8

Published in England by:
James Currey Ltd.
54b Thornhill Square
Islington, London N1 1BE

Contents

vi   *Contents*

Editorial

This issue of *African Literature Today* is entirely devoted to African women writers and the presentation of women in African literature. This in itself is a recognition of two important facts: first, that African women writers, as a number of articles in the collection point out, have been neglected in the largely male-authored journals, critical studies and critical anthologies and, secondly, that the last ten years or so have seen a tremendous blossoming of highly accomplished works by African women writers and it would have been inexcusable to continue to ignore them. The second fact partly, though not entirely, offers an explanation for the first. If the critical attention has been scanty, it is partly because up to the end of the 1960s the literary output of African women was also rather scanty. This is most probably due to a number of well known historical and sociological factors. Writing and education go hand in hand and for all kinds of sociological and other reasons the education of women in Africa lagged far behind that of men. In real terms also, men probably had more leisure to devote to activities like writing, since women had to cope with the enormous tasks of childbearing and childrearing and caring for their men. Furthermore, the African writer as we have come to know him is inevitably a public figure adopting a public stance, functioning as the eye, the conscience and at times the intelligence of his people, assuming the role of a prophet or sage or seer. Adetokunbo Pearce's article on Efua Sutherland's plays suggests precisely how public the role of the dramatist could be and usually is. But African societies have been slow in according to women this 'senior' position and public exposure. In this regard it might seem strange, perhaps, that the genre in which African women have featured least is that of poetry, which is the most private of the genres. The fact remains, however, that in so far as Africa is concerned, the role of the poet also has always been public. The dearth of African women writers, up till the very recent past, is therefore probably in itself a consequence of traditional African attitudes towards women.

Running throughout these articles is the recurrent refrain that women (both African and non-African) and the cause of womanhood have been very inadequately served by African male writers in their works. There is the suggestion that African male writers are either unable or unwilling to present woman in her totality, and have therefore resorted to the use of stereotypes; and that their treatment of issues that most deeply concern women – issues such as polygamy, childbearing, motherhood, the subordination of the female to the male – has been jaundiced. It is only with the advent of women writers, the view goes, that women begin to be adequately treated and women-related issues begin to be objectively analysed. There is some truth in this, but there is also some oversimplification. While it is true that most male writers have not been able to communicate to us how women feel on the burning issues of polygamy, motherhood and relations between the sexes and have simply presented the traditional picture of the woman cosily accepting her lot, it is not true to say that all male writers have been unsympathetic towards women, or have lacked the ability to present truly complex women, or have merely given us stereotypes. As the articles by Sylvia Bryan and Jennifer Evans show, Wole Soyinka, Sembène Ousmane and Ngugi wa Thiong'o are outstanding in their presentation of truly complex women; women who are resourceful, determined and resilient and who, when necessary, break through the barriers imposed by tradition on their sex, with their creators' full endorsement, and take their stand by their men. However, maybe in the final analysis, even these women are merely shown as giving powerful support to their men, and it is left to the women writers, as Katherine Frank says, to present female characters with 'a destiny of their own'.

All this suggests not only that it is in the pages of the African woman writer that we first find an objective treatment of womanhood and the problems of womanhood but also that the African woman writer has a duty to correct misconceptions about women (just as the African writer in the 1950s had a duty to correct the misconceptions and rewrite the stereotypes propagated by the European writer about Africa) and give the genuine woman's point of view on all these issues. Hence the notion of the 'commitment' of the female writer which Molara Ogundipe-Leslie provocatively discusses in her article. Certainly all these tasks need to be undertaken by African women writers. But a note of caution must be sounded. The emphasis on commitment can easily become prescriptive in the sense that we might be telling African women

writers what they must do and there might be a consequent predictability about their works. Just as some critics complained that
it was possible to predict the concerns of almost every African
novel of the 1950s and 1960s, so it might be possible to forecast the
themes of works by African women writers. In fact, by giving the
female point of view on issues like polygamy, marriage, love,
motherhood and relations between the sexes in general, writers
like Mariama Bâ, Aminata Sow Fall and Ama Ata Aidoo have con-
siderably extended the range of the novel's concerns and we can
surely hope that the day will come when, having put all this behind
her, having corrected the misconceptions and set the record
straight, the African woman writer will be free to follow her creative impulse and write about what she pleases.

There is a further implication in most of these articles that the
African woman writer herself has not been adequately served by
male critics. (We note the refreshing preponderance of female
critics in this collection.) And once more it is significant that there
is a similarity here between the position of the woman writer vis-
à-vis the male critic and that of the African writer in the 1960s
vis-à-vis the European or Eurocentric critic, which suggests that
the same problems will arise when literature by a new and hitherto
deprived body of people emerges. It is suggested that one kind of
male critic, failing to realize perhaps that the work of women
writers should not be forced into the male-dominated tradition –
the tradition of the 'other' as Mineke Schipper calls it in her article
– displays a lack of flexibility in his critical approach and studies
these works from a wrong body of assumptions. Certainly we must
preserve a *certain* flexibility and open-mindedness in our approach
to African women writers; we must be honestly prepared to enjoy
and evaluate what we find in their works. But a second note of
caution must be sounded. It might amount to the height of con-
descension (and the feminists themselves will be the first to point
this out) to imply that a different set of critical criteria must be
applied to women's writing, for this might easily degenerate into
the feeling that writing by women is inferior to that by men and will
not easily stand up to the rigorous standards expected of the latter.
This of course would be a completely wrong-headed judgement.
The recent writings of Mariama Bâ, Aminata Sow Fall, Buchi
Emecheta, Ama Ata Aidoo and others suggest that the works of
most of the women can more than hold their own in comparison
with those of their male counterparts, and we need make no allow-
ances for them. The articles by Adetokunbo Pearce and Arlene

Elder demonstrate the complex artistry that underlies some of these works. Furthermore, to suggest that we must place the women writers in a separate 'women's' tradition would be a 'covert way' as Mineke Schipper suggests, of 'keeping them out of the official circuit', out of the male-dominated tradition. Some male African writers have gone down on record as saying that they would wish to be known simply as 'writers' not as 'African writers'. Maybe they overstated their case. But perhaps, when the dust has settled and the air cleared, we should all look forward to the day when the African woman writer would want to be known simply as an African writer, for this would imply, not that she has not paid attention to women's issues, but that she is part of the African literary tradition and that her works, compared with those of her male counterpart, leave nothing to be desired.

The next issue will be *Poetry in African Literature Today*
*Proposals for articles should be sent with a brief summary to the
Editor, Professor Eldred Durosimi Jones:*
Fourah Bay College
University of Sierra Leone
P.O. Box 87
Freetown
Sierra Leone
*All articles should be well typed preferably on A4 paper and double
spaced. References to books should include the author or editor,
place of publication, publisher, date and the relevant pages.*

Bessie Head died on 17 April 1986 at the age of 48. Born in South Africa, the product of a forbidden alliance across lines of colour, she experienced a displaced childhood, a broken marriage, and the hazards of life as a coloured person in her native country. She chose exile in rural Botswana where she distilled her own sufferings and that of others into novels – *When Rainclouds Gather* (1969), *Maru* (1971), *A Question of Power* (1974) and short stories – *The Collector of Treasures* (1977). She also published a valuable historical document, a collection of interviews with the people of Serowe, which pictures the life of her adopted people through three periods of their history. Her deep explorations of mental suffering, the plight of the down-trodden and despised – women and the Bushmen – with sensitiveness and beautiful perception give her a special place in African literature.

Eds.

The Female Writer and Her Commitment[1]

Molara Ogundipe-Leslie

Does the female writer have any particular commitment as a female? What could this possibly be? We shall try to answer this question through a discussion of issues surrounding her commitment. We shall also consider only creative writers.

Feminists have posited that the woman writer has these two major responsibilities; first to tell about being a woman; secondly, to describe reality from a woman's view, a woman's perspective. These two postulations immediately give rise to other questions. What is a woman? What is being a woman and what is the nature of womanhood? These may sound like obvious and ridiculous truisms but we will soon find that the concept of a woman is complex and differs from society to society. Men of careless thought are prone to say: 'Oh, we know what a woman is! She is a being with breasts and female genitalia', but this conception is only one aspect of womanhood.

True, the biological identity of a woman counts and is real. But woman, contrary to what some men (and most) think, is more than 'a biological aperture' as Anaïs Nin said.[2] Woman's biology is indeed an important and necessary aspect of her but it is not all she is and it should not be used to limit her. Not only has woman's biology been made her destiny over the ages, it has given rise to stereotypic notions of the nature of women. Mary Ellman has written about these stereotypes in her book, *Thinking About Women*.[3] Her list of imputed female attributes includes formlessness, passivity, instability, confinement, piety, materiality, spirituality, irrationality, compliancy; and two incorrigible figures: the shrew and the witch. Orthodox or mainstream American literary criticism can boast of works on female stereotypes not necessarily by feminists. The eminent critic Leslie Fiedler discusses the female nature while he interprets a few works by women in his *Love and Death in the American Novel*.[4] In this work, he adds images of the woman as the Rose and the Lily to the list of classic American female stereotypes in literature. Other classic stereotypes in American literature are the 'Earth Mother', and the 'Great American Bitch'.

What are our own female stereotypes in African literature? It would be a worthwhile literary activity to begin to identify them. A brief attempt here will show that we already have the stereotyping of women in African literature. There is the figure of the 'sweet mother', the all-accepting creature of fecundity and self-sacrifice. This figure is often conflated with Mother Africa, with eternal and abstract Beauty and with inspiration, artistic or otherwise as in much francophone poetry, particularly that of Léopold Sédar Senghor and David Diop. The figure of Beauty is not unrelated to the stereotype of the woman as the passionate and sensual lover. Much African poetry concerns itself with the eroticism of the African woman to the extent that it can be argued that many male writers conceive of women only as phallic receptacles. This writer once had to do a radio programme on the image of women in Africa through poetry. Searching through the anthology *Poems of Black Africa*,[5] she found only the image of woman as lover; a great deal of the poetry was about the love of women, not love in its larger sense but sexual, physical love. There was little about the deeper aspects of love such as loyalty, care, kindness, or nurturing. The woman was mainly conceived of as 'mother' or 'erotic lover'. The 'mother' stereotype leads to the limiting of a woman's potential in society. How this affects the female writer will be seen later. The falseness of the myth of motherhood has been demonstrated by Buchi Emecheta in her *Joys of Motherhood* (1979). The way African writers enthuse about motherhood, one wonders if there are no women who hate childbirth or have undeveloped maternal instincts.

In addition to 'the mother' and 'houri' stereotype of the African woman, we may consider the stereotypes of the 'sophisticated' city girl and the rural woman. The two are often contrasted in order to dramatize the conflict of modernity and traditionalism. Both figures are often shallow, exaggerated and false. The sophisticated woman is shown as completely divorced from life in the country or from relatives and friends who are not living in her city or sharing her night life. Very often she is a prostitute,[6] an early and recurrent figure in African literature since Abdoulaye Sadji's *Maïmouna, la petite fille noire* (1953) and Cyprian Ekwensi's *Jagua Nana* (1961). The 'sophisticated' woman, like Okot p'Bitek's Clementina, co-wife of Lawino in *Song of Lawino* (1966) is an unreal being. Counter-poised to this 'city girl' is the rural woman, another mirage, the 'pot of culture' who is static as history passes her by, who wants the old ways of life, who speaks like a lobotomized idiot about 'iron snakes' (railways) and 'our husband'. This naive-sounding woman who does not want change and is happy with no innovation does not exist in the African countryside. Lawino is one such. She is one such impossible and unlikely image of the rural woman. In fact, this writer would like to submit that *Song of Lawino* is one of the most critically neglected works in African literature. Overwhelmed by the book's lyricism and the startling use of fresh images, we all enthused over the work on its appearance. But it can be very seriously faulted, as I hope to show later, in another place, for its total conception of existence, culture, African history and the needs of modern Africa. It should be faulted for its unhistorical view of culture, its simplification of Acholi culture and its philosophical yearning for 'a state of nature' that does not adequately describe Acholi culture or indeed most African cultures. It is the mission-educated man's vision of Africa. But, to proceed, what rural woman can be as 'dumb' as Lawino! What rural woman can react, see and speak like Lawino, the wife of a university lecturer in Makerere or Nairobi who nevertheless talks like an idiot about modern things, reacts so naively to a clock and longs for the village verities that Okot also fondly longs for! The figure of Lawino is a displacement from the mind of a *male*, Westernized writer just as Okot's Malaya is a man's view of how a prostitute thinks, speaks or dreams.

Unfortunately, it is not only African male writers who are guilty of this kind of mythification of the rural woman. One feels the same way about the rural woman in Ama Ata Aidoo's *No Sweetness Here* (1970). For after all the felicities and elegance of her narra-tive style and her just social perceptions, one wonders whether the rural woman actually speaks and thinks so naively and limitedly; so childishly. Is the rendering not the educated person's view of what the rural person sees, notes, values and cares about? The truth is that the rural woman wants change and innovation. She wants power, wealth and status like the men. She wants to ride a car rather than walk; use plastics or metal instead of calabashes; use a gas or electric stove instead of firewood, despite all our middle-class nostalgia for that past. After all, we only need these ways of life on our postcards and Christmas cards to send abroad to our oh-so-intellectual friends. We do not have to live in a smoke-filled hut! And it seems that the African male needs this myth to buoy-up his conservatism and his yearning for that pre-colonial patriarchal past where he was definitely king as father, husband and ruler. The myth of the unchanging, naive rural woman seems to coincide with the actual social practice and tendency of men to discourage change and innovation in women's lives. In an anthropological study of East African women and their struggle for economic independence which often takes the forms of hard work, transactional manipulation and urban migration, Christine Obbo concludes that:

> even though the world is changing all about them, it seems that women's own attempts to cope with the new situations they find themselves in are regarded as a 'problem' by men, and a betrayal of traditions which are often confused with women's roles. *Women must act as mediators between the past and the present, while men see themselves as mediators between the present and the future.* This seems to be part of the reason behind opposition to female migration. The forces of urbanization and international influences have imposed rapid changes upon East African societies, yet men expect women to be politically conservative and non-innovative. Socially, women are accused of 'going too far' when they adopt new practices usually emanating ultimately from the capitals of the metropolitan countries.[7]

One of the commitments of the female writer should be to the correction of these false images of the woman in Africa. To do this, she herself must know the reality of the African woman, must know the truth about African women and womanhood. I have said earlier that the concept of a woman is a complex one. Womanhood does not only relate to gender, because situations exist where women adopt other gender roles (although sometimes only after menopause) as with women in the armies of Dahomey in the eighteenth and nineteenth centuries, women who marry wives in Igboland and lord it over the husbands of their acquired wives and women who are called 'men' when they attain certain levels of economic and social independence. Among the Enuani Western Igbo, women who are professionally liberated, such as owners of theatre troupes or poets, and women who are financially independent and strong in character are named 'men'.[8] In that society, the conception of a woman varies, depending on the institutions within which she is being considered; political, marital, professional or economic. The female writer must tell us about being a woman in the real complex sense of the term.

On the biological level, she must tell us about being a woman:

what the facts of menstruation, pregnancy, childbirth and menopause contribute to the woman's personality and the way she feels and knows her world. Do women's bodies affect their senses, their use of imagery, their personal writing styles? Debates on these considerations have taken place in European literary criticism involving women such as Charlotte Brontë, George Eliot, Virginia Woolf, George Sand and Anaïs Nin among others. Male writers have also had their own 'phallic' or 'phallocratique' contributions to make. We need to know the African female writers' views more directly. Male African writers have from time to time given their artistic reactions to female experiences such as menstruation, sexual love, and childbirth among others, but a female writer's view would be more authentic. The theme of childlessness has been explored by African female writers so much that one would wish they would seek other themes.[9] But much remains to be said in the area of female biological experience. Even the sensitive and beautiful *So Long a Letter* (1981) by Mariama Bâ does not explore the personal, physical areas of the women's relationships to their loves. There, Bâ becomes very abstract and poetic, almost mystical. What did Ramatoulaye feel to be sexually abandoned by Moudou? How did she feel at nights? How did Aissatou survive in New York as the critic, Femi Ojo-Ade, has asked?[10]

But to enquire about the female biological experience is not to posit that there is a feminine nature, immanent and recurrent, that can be used to identify all females and thus pigeon-hole them as has been done in history. Simone de Beauvoir as early as 1953 in the history of radical feminism gave short shrift to this notion in her long and laboriously scientific discussion of the woman as the second sex.[11] She argues that it is absurd to speak of 'woman' in general as of the 'eternal man'. She submits that there is no feminine nature, only a feminine situation that has in many respects remained constant through the centuries and that largely determines the character of its victims. The notion of 'femininity' (to be distinguished from 'femaleness' – my insertion) is a fiction invented by men, assented to by women untrained in the rigours of logical thought or conscious of the advantages to be gained from compliance with masculine fantasies. To quote Patricia Spack's summary of Simone de Beauvoir's position:

> Their assent traps them in the prison of repetition and immanence which limits woman's possibilities. Man reserves for himself the terrors and triumphs of transcendence; he offers woman safety, the temptations of passivity and acceptance; he tells her that passivity and

acceptance are her nature. Simone de Beavoir tells her that that is a lie, that her nature is complicated and various, that she must escape, liberate herself, shape her own future, deny the myths that confine her.[12]

The socialization of women is certainly very important here. The European notion of femininity is even less applicable to Africa where women have adopted all kinds of roles not considered feminine in Europe. The wife of Amos Tutuola's Palm-Wine Drinkard is one of the best and most correct images of the Yoruba woman of all classes: a courageous, resourceful woman who dares situations with her husband, who works at anything and willingly changes roles with him, where the need arises.

To restate, what then is the commitment of the African female writer in view of the above? The female writer should be committed in three ways: as a <u>writer</u>, as a <u>woman</u> and as a <u>Third World person</u>; and her biological womanhood is implicated in all three. As a writer, she has to be committed to her art, seeking to do justice to it at the highest levels of expertise. She should be committed to her vision, whatever it is, which means she has to be willing to stand or fall for that vision. She must tell her own truth, and write what she wishes to write. But she must be certain that what she is telling is the truth and nothing but – albeit her own truth. Most African female writers are committed to their art by being conscious craftswomen, though their skill varies in quality from person to person. For formal ingenuity, we could name: Bessie Head, Ama Ata Aidoo, Mariama Bâ in the genre of fiction; Efua Sutherland, Aidoo, 'Zulu Sofola and Micere Mugo in drama and poetry. One is struck by the paucity of female poets. (Are there genres that are particularly attractive to and malleable by women?) There were English critics and writers who believed that fiction was the proper genre for a women writer. George Henry Lewis, the 'consort' of George Eliot, certainly believed that. But there are even fewer playwrights – about five. Why is this? Could it be that being a playwright implies production; working in a theatre, after hours, at all hours, in the company of men? Such a profession would be a source of insecurity for some husbands. I have known a male playwright who withdrew his actress wife from the theatre!

Committed to their art African female writers definitely are. But being committed to their womanhood is another matter and a problematic one. Being committed to one's womanhood would necessitate taking up the tasks discussed earlier in this essay. It would mean delineating the experience of women as women, telling what it is to be a woman, destroying male stereotypes of women. But many of the African female writers like to declare that they are not feminists, as if it were a crime to be a feminist. These denials come from unlikely writers such as Bessie Head,[13] Buchi Emecheta,[14] even Mariama Bâ.[15] I would put this down to the successful intimidation of African women by men over the issues of women's liberation and feminism. Male ridicule, aggression and backlash have resulted in making women apologetic and have given the term 'feminist' a bad name. Yet, nothing could be more feminist than the writings of these women writers, in their concern for and deep understanding of the experiences and fates of women in society.

That the female writer should be committed to her Third World reality and status may lead to disagreements. Being aware of oneself as a Third World person implies being politically conscious, offering readers perspectives on and perceptions of colonialism, imperialism and neo-colonialism as they affect and shape our lives and historical destinies. Most apolitical writers and critics would baulk at this and claim their illusory freedoms, their 'Hyde Park Corner' freedom, as an Egyptian writer and activist, Nawal el Saadawy calls it. They would argue that they need not be forced to be political. But any true intelligence in Africa must note the circumscription of our lives here by the 'reality of imperialism and neo-colonialism'. Perhaps only Ama Ata Aidoo and Micere Mugo can be said to be thus politically conscious. Yet, in spite of the fact that most of the writers would not speak about political economy, they do tend to believe in art for a purpose, in tendentious art, so to speak. Statements have been made, in their various interviews, about the educative nature of art, while the term 'education' is itself used in various and broad senses: in the directly educational manner of Efua Sutherland's plays for children; as the education of sensibility and ethical awareness in the writings of Bessie Head; as the education of Africans about their traditional culture and their present-day problems in the works of 'Zulu Sofola, Mariama Bâ, Aminata Sow Fall, Grace Ogot and Rebeka Njau, to name but a few. Flora Nwapa and Buchi Emecheta certainly wish to educate us about the woman's realm of experience, while the women writers of Southern Africa – Angola, Mozambique and South Africa – of which nine have been counted in the works of David Herdeck and of Hans Zell, Carol Bundy and Virginia Coulon, wish to educate us about apartheid and the shaping influences in their strife-torn countries.[16]

This writer feels that the female writers cannot usefully claim to be concerned with various social predicaments in their countries or in Africa without situating their awareness and solutions within the larger global context of imperialism and neo-colonialism. For what is it that makes us so dismally poor? What forced our individuals into such schizophrenic cultural confusion? Why are the national ruling classes so irresponsible, criminal and wasteful? Because they have sold out? To whom? A deep female writer who has anything worthwhile to say must have these insights.

Is there anything that recommends the female writer more particularly to this socially educative role? There is the myth that women are more ethically ferocious than men, and more reliable. (This is why they are always voted to be treasurers in Nigerian organizations!) William Thackeray among other nineteenth-century critics certainly thought so when he spoke of 'the passionate honour of the woman'. Certainly, nineteenth-century European and American women's fiction, (most of which was by women, anyway) was impelled by various kinds of moral impetuses: Jane Austen and the limitations of marriage for the woman; the Brontës and the torments of independent women in society; Mrs Gaskell and her concerns for the working class; Harriet Beecher Stowe and slavery in America; Harriet Martineau and economic and social questions in England; and George Sand and the search for social justice and socialism in France.[17] Does the African female writer have any moral prerogative to point the way to others and educate the spirit? And why? As mothers, more experienced sufferers or more sentient and ethical beings?

NOTES

1. Editor's note: An earlier version of this article appeared in *The Guardian* (Lagos), 21 December 1983.
2. Anaïs Nin, selections in J. Goulianos (ed.), *By A Woman Writt*, London, Penguin, 1973, p. 299. Born in Paris in 1903 of Cuban and Danish parents, Anaïs Nin was taken to the United States by her mother in 1914. She lived in France intermittently in the 1920s and between 1930 and 1940 when she was a member of the Parisian literary circle that included Henry Miller and Lawrence Durrell. In 1940 she moved to the United States where she died in 1977. She is famous for her *Diary* which runs into over 150 manuscript volumes. She observes:

'The woman artist has to create something different from man. . . . She has to sever herself from the myth man creates, from being created by him, she has to struggle with her own cycles, storms, terrors which man does not understand' (Goulianos, p. 291).

3. Mary Ellman, *Thinking About Women*, New York, Harcourt Brace Jovanovich, 1968.
4. Leslie Fiedler, *Love and Death in the American Novel*, New York, Stein and Day, 1966.
5. Wole Soyinka (ed.), *Poems of Black Africa*, London, Heinemann, 1975.
6. The use of the prostitute figure has been given a book-length study by Senkoro of Tanzania. See F.E.M.K. Senkoro, *The Prostitute in African Literature*, Dar es Salaam, Dar es Salaam University Press, 1982. Senkoro identifies backward and progressive uses of the prostitute figure in literature.
7. Christine Obbo, *African Woman: Their Struggle for Economic Independence*, London, Zed Press, 1980, p. 143.
8. Conversation with 'Zulu Sofola, female playwright, 29 November, 1983.
9. The theme of childlessness has been treated in the following works: Flora Nwapa, *Efuru*, London, Heinemann, 1966; *Idu*, London, Heinemann, 1979; *One is Enough*, Enugu, Tana Press, 1981. Buchi Emecheta, *The Joys of Motherhood*, London, Heinemann, 1979. Ama Ata Aidoo, *Anowa*, London, Longman, 1980. Chuma Ifedi, *Behind the Clouds*, London, Longman, 1981.
10. Femi Ojo-Ade, 'Female Writers, Male Critics', *African Literature Today*, 13, London, Heinemann, 1982, pp. 158–79.
11. Simone de Beauvoir, *The Second Sex*, New York, Knopf, 1953.
12. Patricia Meyer Spacks, *The Female Imagination*, New York, Avon Books, 1976, p. 17.
13. See the biography of Bessie Head in Hans Zell, Carol Bundy and Virginia Coulon (eds), *A New Reader's Guide to African Literature*, London, Heinemann, 1983.
14. See biography in ibid.
15. See biography in ibid.
16. ibid.;   D. Herdeck, *African Authors: A Companion To Black African Writing – Volume I: 1300–1973*, Washington, DC, Black Orpheus, 1973. In all, this writer has been able to count thirty-two female writers in these two reference works. Twenty-five write fiction, long and short; five write plays while seven write poetry. Some writers write in more than one genre.
17. For a very informative study of the place and achievement of nineteenth-century women writers, see Ellen Moers, *Literary Women: The Great Writers*, New York, Doubleday; Anchor Books, 1977, in particular Chapter 2, 'The Epic Age: Part of the History of Literary Women' and Chapter 3, 'Women's Literary Traditions and the Individual Talent'.

Women Without Men: The Feminist Novel in Africa

Katherine Frank

If the Victorian novel invariably closed with a wedding, the contemporary British or American novel almost as inevitably opens with a divorce, especially if the novelist is a woman: ten or fifteen years have passed since 'happily ever after', the 'angel in the house' is restless and unhappy, her children well on the way to being grown, their father a tyrant or stranger or perhaps just a bore. In a pattern that goes back to Ibsen's *A Doll's House*, our heroine slams the door on her domestic prison, journeys out into the great world, slays the dragons of her patriarchal society, and triumphantly discovers the grail of feminism by 'finding herself'. The quest motif, in short, and we have met the feminist pilgrim countless times in the past decade or so in the best-selling novels of such writers as Doris Lessing, Margaret Drabble, Erica Jong, and Marilyn French. Indeed, the pattern has become by now something of a literary cliché, and yet each year brings a new crop of the same. Whatever their aesthetic merits or defects may be, these books reflect a widespread social reality in the West, and they clearly answer the needs of countless women experiencing that reality painfully and at first hand.

With its peculiarly Western orientation toward individualism and self-fulfilment and its simultaneous exploration of patriarchal oppression and the female struggle for freedom, one might gather that this feminist scenario would hold little relevance for the African novel. Until recently most African novels have been written by men, and they tend to focus on social, historical, and political rather than personal or domestic themes. By and large women characters are defined in these novels by their relations to men: they are someone's daughter or wife or mother, shadowy figures who hover on the fringes of the plot, suckling infants, cooking, plaiting their hair. Or, as Kenneth Little has shown in detail, women in male-authored African novels tend to fall into a specific category of female stereotypes: girlfriends or good-time girls, workers such as secretaries or clerks, wives and other male appendages, and prostitutes or courtesans.[1] Of course, there are exceptions to such stereotyped characterization; in Sembène Ousmane's *God's Bits of Wood*, for example, or nearly all the novels of Nuruddin Farah. But the fact remains that we need to turn to the growing number of women novelists in Africa in order to find female characters with a destiny of their own.

And it turns out to be a destiny with a vengeance as the most recent novels by Mariama Bâ, Flora Nwapa, Buchi Emecheta, and Ama Ata Aidoo all show. The feminist novel in Africa is not only alive and well, it is, in general, more radical, even more militant, than its Western counterpart. It lacks the Utopian flavour of many American or British efforts; books such as Emecheta's *Double Yoke* or Nwapa's *One is Enough* do not dabble in daydreaming about enlightened heroes or reformed, non-sexist societies. There is a bitterness and cynicism born of the unflinching vision and hard struggle that informs these books. Furthermore, one is struck by the magnitude of their repudiation. All these novels embrace the solution of a world without men: man is the enemy, the exploiter and oppressor. Given the historically established and culturally sanctioned sexism of African society, there is no possibility of a compromise, or even truce with the enemy. Instead, women must spurn patriarchy in all its guises and create a safe, sane, supportive world of women: a world of mothers and daughters, sisters, and friends. This, of course, amounts to feminist separatism, though only obliquely in Aidoo's *Our Sister Killjoy* do we find the logical outcome of this ideology; lesbianism.

The militancy of the new feminist novel in Africa, then, arises from the institutionalized sexism of contemporary African life, though there is endless debate among writers, critics, journalists, sociologists, and anthropologists over whether this entrenched patriarchal culture came with the white colonialists or is inherent in African society. Flora Nwapa and Ama Ata Aidoo hold that it derives from the white man or, more accurately, from the white man's wife and her helpless, dependent, unproductive life in the colonies. According to this view, the European imperialists – along with all their other political and social impositions – also brought the norm of feminine subordination in the face of masculine power and oppression. Writers such as Buchi Emecheta and the critic Lloyd Brown, however, disagree and reject in Brown's words, 'the image of the free-spirited and independent African woman whose problems, as woman, have flowed from colonialism rather than indigenous mores.' This false image, Brown goes on to say, 'is bandied from seminar to seminar, and conference to conference, until it has become one of the . . . enduring clichés of African studies everywhere: "the African woman doesn't need to be liberated because she's already liberated".'[2]

It is probably impossible to settle once and for all this long-standing debate over whether African women were better off in a traditional, usually rural, milieu or whether they are happier and more autonomous in today's Westernized urban centres. The evidence of anthropology is mixed. On the one hand, for example, Enid Schildkrout has demonstrated the economic independence of traditional Hausa women in purdah,[3] while Carmel Dinan has written graphically of the empty lives of nominally liberated white-collar single women in Accra who live comfortable, often luxurious lives, surrounded by all manner of Western gadgets provided by older 'sugar daddies' who shower material goods on their girfriends in exchange for sexual services.[4] And so it remains a vexed issue, and clearly all the sociological and literary votes on this question of the source, nature, and extent of the oppression of women in Africa are not yet in.

When we look at African feminist novels, however, it is striking to note that all of them have educated, highly Westernized heroines, and all are set in urban environments. Specifically, I am thinking of five books published in the last few years: Mariama Bâ's *So Long a Letter* (1980), Flora Nwapa's *One is Enough* (1981), Buchi Emecheta's *Double Yoke* (1982) and *Destination Biafra* (1982), and Ama Ata Aidoo's *Our Sister Killjoy* (1977). The feminist heroines in these books all have the professional and economic means to live without men and they do so in an urban world which will at least accommodate, if not encourage, their anomalous single status. That their situation is a very new and still tenuous one is shown in the recurring conflict between mothers and daughters in, for example, *One is Enough, Destination Biafra*, and *Double Yoke*. The heroines' mothers in these books embody traditional African values and in their incomprehension and dismay at their daughters' behaviour – their disapproval, for example, when their daughters smoke and wear trousers – they reinforce the patriarchal values of African society. Like their daughters' suitors and husbands, these mothers want to see their daughters securely married and perpetually pregnant. They cannot imagine a destiny for their daughters other than the one they have endured, a destiny portentously expressed by an editorial in the Ghanaian *Daily Graphic*: 'A woman may gain the whole world but she would have lost her soul if she doesn't become a male's extension or somebody's mother.'[5]

To flout the ideals not merely of one's society but also of one's own mother is a very difficult and sometimes heartbreaking task. Thus, even given their education and an urban environment responsive to their aspirations, the plight of these young women is a lonely, difficult, and often immensely sad one. As Maria Rosa Cutrefelli puts it in *Women of Africa: The Roots of Oppression*:

> the new characteristically urban figure of the male-unprotected, husbandless single woman has significantly taken shape: and in the light of the traditional view of celibacy as a social failure, even a crime against society, the consciously deliberate rejection of marriage on the part of an increasing number of urban women appears to be a courageous, indeed a daring deed.[6]

Central to such 'heroism', to use Ellen Moers's term in *Literary Women*, is the Western notion of individualism. And herein lies the real source of conflict implicit in African feminism. For feminism is by definition an individualistic ideology in contrast to the communal nature of African society. Beatrice Stegeman sets up the dichotomy in an article on the 'New Woman' in male-authored African literature when she remarks that 'communalism implies a standard of value of submergence rather than self-realization. In traditional African societies, the role of each citizen is to perpetuate the status quo, to assume continuity of the clan, to work within tradition, and to maintain the closed society.'[7] In contrast:

> the New Woman represents a theory of personhood where the individual exists as an independent entity rather than her kinship relations, where she has a responsibility to realize her potential for happiness rather than to accept her role, where she has indefinable value rather than quantitative financial worth, and where she must reason about her own values rather than fit into a stereotyped tradition.[8]

In human terms this means that the New Woman in Africa often wavers helplessly between her allegiance to her culture – her African identity – and her aspiration for freedom and self-fulfilment. Time and again in these novels we encounter women characters who have internalized the clash between Western and African values that pertains in the larger society. As Charlotte Bruner notes in her Introduction to a new anthology of writing by African women, 'often they show their female protagonists as torn, confused, in a milieu of cross-cultural conflict.'[9] The paramount question that nearly all these novels pose, in fact, is how can this conflict be resolved, how can the contemporary African woman negotiate her way between the claims of tradition and modernization, how, finally, can she be rendered whole again?

This question is perhaps articulated most powerfully in Mariama Bâ's *So Long a Letter* and Flora Nwapa's *One is Enough*. Both novels involve the painful, faltering, but ultimately successful movement of a woman from a traditional African world to a very different, Westernized urban life. In both cases, the precipitating factor in the 'consciousness raising' process of the books' heroines is the brutal imposition of polygamy. Polygamy, of course, is the most glaringly inequitable and sexist feature of traditional African society. After thirty years of marriage and twelve children, Ramatoulaye, the heroine of *So Long a Letter*, is devastated when her husband takes as a second wife the schoolmate of one of their daughters. The novel consists of a long lament and meditation on the pain, anger, and despair Ramatoulaye suffers as a result of her husband's desertion, and it is addressed to her closest friend, Aissatou, who not long before had divorced her husband when he also took a second wife.

On one level the book is a celebration of female bonding, of Ramatoulaye and Aissatou's enduring friendship, of their shared world without men. As Ramatoulaye says, 'the essential thing is the content of our hearts which animates us; the essential thing is the quality of the sap that flows through us. You have often proved to me the superiority of friendship over love.'[10] In a sense, then, Ramatoulaye's 'so long a letter' is a love letter to her dearest friend.

But it also seems to be addressed to herself as well as to Aissatou; a kind of internal monologue charting the painful process of her liberation. For Aissatou embodies the self that Ramatoulaye is struggling to become. This is shown clearly in their very different reactions to their husbands taking second wives. Without hesitating a moment, Aissatou walks out on her husband, leaving as explanation a defiant letter which ends, 'I am stripping myself of your love, your name. Clothed in my dignity, the only worthy garment, I go my way'. (p. 32). Ramatoulaye, in contrast, assumes the posture of the traditional, obedient African wife and submits to her husband's second marriage. In her 'cri de coeur' she confesses to her friend, 'I ask myself questions. The truth is that, despite everything, I remain faithful to the love of my youth. Aissatou, I cry for Modou and I can do nothing about it.' (p. 56). Despite Ramatoulaye's acquiescence, Modou abandons her and their children entirely, so the cost of her submission is enormous: 'But my despair persists,' she writes Aissatou, 'but my rancour remains, but the waves of an immense sadness break in me.' (p. 12).

Yet slowly, painfully, with her friend's and daughters' support and encouragement, Ramatoulaye comes to terms with her involuntary single state. Hers is not, as is the case with the other heroines to be considered, a willed or chosen freedom. But gradually she begins to use and even enjoy it. She 'survives', as she reports to Aissatou. She learns how to do all the shopping by herself, to pay the electricity and water bills, to replace locks and latches, to deal with the plumber, all the while keeping up with her job as a teacher and the needs and demands of her twelve children. Initially the struggle is merely to meet the basic material requirements and demands of family life. But soon she begins going to the cinema alone; she continues to be a voracious reader and from both books and films she 'learned ... lessons of greatness, courage, and perseverance' (p. 52). Finally Aissatou, who is a well-off embassy official in the United States, gives Ramatoulaye a car, a highly symbolic gift. The Fiat brings Ramatoulaye mobility and freedom; it enables her to transport herself and the children. When she learns how to drive Ramatoulaye assumes control of her new life and the direction in which she wishes to travel.

At the end of the novel Ramatoulaye and Aissatou are on the verge of being reunited when Aissatou returns to Senegal for a holiday from the United States. As the book progresses, we watch Ramatoulaye move closer and closer to the 'role model' of her dearest friend, so it is appropriate that the story concludes by actually bringing them together again in their warm female friendship, consisting of equal measures of love, support, respect and admiration. And their meeting will also symbolize the crucial union of Westernized, feminist fulfilment and African culture, as Ramatoulaye suggests when she imagines how Aissatou will look and the meal they will share:

> So, then, will I see you tomorrow in a tailored suit or a long dress? I've taken a bet ... tailored suit. Used to living far away, you will want – again I've taken a bet ... table, plate, chair, fork. More convenient, you

will say. But I will not let you have your way. I will spread out a mat. On it there will be the big, steaming bowl into which you will have to accept that other hands dip. (p. 89)

What is so crucial about the sort of friendship Ramatoulaye and Aissatou share – this world they create apart from men – is that it entirely lacks those qualities of male–female relationships which cause women so much grief: power, restraint, and subordination. Even when one woman is stronger or more powerful than another as is the case with Aissatou and Ramatoulaye, she does not wield her power over her weaker sister. In fact, the exact opposite occurs: power is used by the stronger to support and strengthen the weaker. Aissatou does all she can to lift Ramatoulaye out of her despair and dependence, to make her autonomous and whole again. So what could be more fitting than the book closing with the reunion of these two oldest and closest of friends. On the eve of Aissatou's arrival Ramatoulaye also shows how very far she has travelled with Aissatou's support, 'I am not indifferent to the irreversible currents of women's liberation that are lashing the world. This commotion that is shaking up every aspect of our lives reveals and illustrates our abilities. My heart rejoices each time a woman emerges from the shadows' (p. 88). Ramatoulaye herself has finally emerged from the shadows. She closes her long letter with her name, badly written, which up until now the reader has not even known. The name represents the attainment at long last of Ramatoulaye's hard-earned struggle for an independent identity. Her signature is her assertion of selfhood.

Like Ramatoulaye, Amaka, the heroine of Flora Nwapa's latest novel, *One is Enough*, also starts off in a state of feminine submission and dependence. The novel opens with her grovelling before her heartless mother-in-law, begging not to be 'thrown away' because she has failed to produce a child in six years of marriage to Obiora. The tragedy of barrenness is a recurring theme in Nwapa's work, going all the way back to her first novel, *Efuru*. In African culture barrenness is perhaps the worst affliction (even crime) a couple can edure (or commit), and it is almost always attributed to the woman. In traditional society for a woman to lack reproductive power is to lack all power, indeed to be deprived of her very identity and 'raison d'être' in life. So fundamental is female fertility to an African woman's social position and self-worth that out of the five radically feminist novels under discussion only two have childless heroines. (And to move parenthetically from art to life, though many contemporary women writers in Africa are unmarried, virtually all of them have children). Reflecting on her fate Amaka thinks, 'God had deprived her of the greatest blessing bestowed on a woman, the joy of being a mother'. And then she goes on to ask 'Was that really the end of the world? Was she useless to the world if she were unmarried?'[11] Much of the novel involves her formulation of negative answers to these questions.

As is the case in *So Long a Letter*, what goads the heroine to action is the intolerable prospect of polygamy. When Obiora takes as a second wife a woman who has already, unbeknownst to Amaka, borne him two sons, Amaka packs up her things and leaves the traditional world of Onitsha for Lagos. Here, at the age of thirty, she begins life anew and soon becomes a prosperous business woman.

For Nwapa the route to liberation is economic power. The novel is dedicated to Nwapa's mother-in-law 'who believes that all women married or single must be economically independent'. In an interview Nwapa has herself insisted on this point when she talks of women from her own background and their business acumen: 'if it means selling oranges, then we sell oranges' to be financially autonomous.[12] Where Bâ sees female solidarity and Emecheta education as the crucial factors underlying women's self-determination, Nwapa believes that unhampered financial prosperity is the key to happiness and success for women. And Amaka quickly succeeds on her author's terms. She gets numerous lucrative contracts, including 3000 naira for supplying toilet rolls and half-a-million naira for building a wall around some barracks.

But the means by which Amaka gets ahead are questionable to say the least, and undermine the validity of her success. By sleeping with a certain Alhaji and – of all people – a Catholic priest, Amaka makes the contacts and gets the contracts she wants. She is quite forthright about her 'modus operandi'. Looking back at all her sufferings in Onitsha during her years as a wife she reflects that 'she did not realize how hurt she was until her eyes were opened in Lagos and she began to see what she could do as a woman, using her bottom power as they say in Nigeria.' (p. 126) 'Bottom power', to call a spade a spade, is really just a shrewd kind of prostitution. Amaka has no illusions about her behaviour: she is being exploited in the most fundamental and time-honoured way. But two things partially redeem her actions. First, she chooses her oppressors and she chooses them carefully to maximize the benefits she gains from her sexual services. And, secondly, she really has very little choice: 'bottom power' seems to be the only way to make it. 'You know Lagos,' Amaka says to her close friend Adaobi, 'no man can do anything for a woman, even if the woman is the wife of a head of state, without asking her for her most precious possession – herself.' (p. 71).

Amaka, then, is a problematic and somewhat disconcerting heroine. On the one hand, she clearly articulates a radical feminist-separatist credo: 'She would find fulfilment, she would find pleasure, even happiness in being a single woman. The erroneous belief that without a husband a woman was nothing must be disproved.' (p. 27). But at the same time she has the materialistic, good-time, rather vulgar desires and values of a Jagua Nana: 'she wanted peace to go about her business, look beautiful, wear good clothes, go to the hairdresser every week, in fact, enjoy life fully.' (p. 24).

Not only does Amaka enjoy life fully, with her three-bedroom bungalow in Lagos and her Peugeot 504, in time she also has twin boys by the Catholic priest. Father McLaid (a Nigerian despite his Irish name) falls in love with Amaka and wants to leave the church and marry her, but she adamantly refuses. She has her babies, her close friend Adaobi, her house and car and business deals. She neither wants nor needs a husband. With perfect, uncompromising self-knowledge she tells McLaid:

> I don't want to be a wife . . . a mistress, yes, with a lover, yes of course, but not a wife. There is something in that word that does not suit me. As a wife, I am never free. I am a shadow of myself. As a wife, I am almost impotent. I am in prison, unable to advance in body or soul. Something gets hold of me as a wife and destroys me. When I rid myself of Obiora, things started working for me. I don't want to go back to my 'wifely' days. No, I am through with husbands. I said farewell to husbands the first day I came to Lagos. (p. 132)

The key words here, I think, are 'shadow' and 'impotent'. Amaka, like the women Ramatoulaye speaks of, wants, indeed has, moved out from the shadows and in doing so has lost the feminine impotence or powerlessness of the traditional African woman she was at the start of the book.

This issue of 'bottom power', prostitution, sexual bargaining – whatever name one wishes to call it by – is also central to Buchi Emecheta's novel *Double Yoke*, though in this case sexual services are rendered not for financial but rather for educational gain.

Emecheta, more than any other woman writer in Africa today, sees education as the most potent means of women's liberation. It is a central theme in all her novels and her heroines are free and fulfilled in direct proportion to the extent of their learning. Education constitutes power in Emecheta's books in two ways. Most obviously, it equips women to be economically independent, to prepare for a job or profession that will enable them to take care of themselves and their children without the help and protection of men. Perhaps just as importantly, though, education also gives women a vision of human experience beyond the narrow confines of their own lives; it bestows a kind of imaginative power, a breadth of perspective, an awareness of beauty, dreams, possibility. This is why books are so important to Emecheta's heroines. Even if they cannot literally escape the imprisoning constraints of their patriarchal world they can imaginatively transcend them through the means of books.

The heroine of *Double Yoke*, Nko, is a student at a Nigerian university much like the University of Calabar where Emecheta recently taught for a year, and *Double Yoke*, among other things, is a clever and absolutely on-target satire on West African academia. But its more serious intention is aptly summed up by the title. Unlike Ramatoulaye and Amaka who move from an oppressive, traditional existence to a new, liberated, autonomous life, Nko labours under the double yoke of tradition and liberation and tries – with ambiguous success – to meet the claims of both. She confides to her mother. 'Oh mother, I want to have both worlds. I want to be an academician and I want to be a quiet, nice and obedient wife. I want the two mothers'. And her mother responds with a sigh, 'daughter you know what you are under, you are under a double yoke'.[13] A little later Nko recognizes the great gulf between these two goals but her determination is still strong: 'she must either have her degree and be a bad, loose, feminist, shameless career woman who would fight men all her life; or do without her degree and be a good, loving wife and Christian woman . . . Oh blast it all! She was going to have both. She was going to manoeuvre these men to give her both' (p. 135).

There are a number of noteworthy things in these two passages. First, the metaphor of the double yoke itself, a heavy, restraining image suggesting cattle or other beasts of burden. Secondly, despite the seeming irreconcilability of her aims, Nko's determination is unabated. And finally, she is going to manoeuvre or manipulate men into giving her what she wants; specifically, she will sleep with the odious, hypocritical Professor Ikot in order to get a first-class honours degree. Nko must indulge in this sexual bargaining, thereby deferring for a while a world without men, because men hold all the power in African society. Women can get what they want only by consorting with the enemy in a kind of psychosexual guerrilla warfare. That men *are* the enemy is clearly shown not only by the behaviour of the predatory Ikot but also by Nko's aggressive, jealous boyfriend, Ete Kamba. In fact, much of the novel is narrated from Ete Kamba's point of view, giving the reader a first-hand view of the African sexist mentality from within. Particularly chilling in this regard are Ete Kamba's thoughts and actions when he has sexual relations with Nko for the first time: it is an act of conquest, even plunder, wholly devoid of tenderness, and afterwards Ete Kamba is obsessed with the fear that Nko may not have been a virgin, thereby robbing him of the spoils of his victory over her.

Given this state of pitched warfare that exists between men and women in *Double Yoke*, the world of the novel is a highly polarized one sexually. There are two camps: Ikot, Ete Kamba and his friends on the one hand, and Nko, her mother, and her room-mates on the other. The story shuttles back and forth between these two realms of male and female experience, and the recurring skirmishes that arise when they collide. With this state of siege it is not surprising that Nko's success is somewhat questionable. She sleeps with Ikot to advance herself academically and she threatens blackmail (Ikot is campaigning to become the next vice-chancellor) if he refuses to help her get a First. She also spurns Ete Kamba when he brands her a whore. And finally, when she learns she is pregnant with Ikot's child, she determines to have the baby and then return to the university and complete her degree. Her plans, then, appear to be to reject both men, keep her child, and succeed academically and professionally on her own terms. But on the final page of the novel Emecheta has 'Fate' disrupt Nko's programme for an autonomous future without men. Her father dies suddenly and in her great grief Nko turns to Ete Kamba and goes back to her village with her boyfriend. It is a strange but perhaps realistic conclusion. Nevertheless, it calls into question everything that Nko has struggled for in the course of the book. *Double Yoke*, in short, poses a problem rather than providing a solution. But despite the uncertainty of its conclusion it clearly demonstrates that women and men in contemporary African society are at war with one another, that women cannot hope to vanquish their oppressors in open combat. Instead, they must cleverly exploit their exploiters and then retreat for their emotional needs to a separatist world of women.

In *Destination Biafra* Emecheta moves from the guerrilla battle of the sexes in *Double Yoke* to the historical and political reality of the Biafran war in Nigeria. It is a daring departure from the domestic preserve of most novels written by African women. *Destination Biafra*, in fact, is probably the only war novel within recent memory written by a woman, and as Emecheta says in her Foreword, 'the subject is as they say, "masculine", but I feel a great sense of . . . achievement in having completed it.'[14]

Not only is this 'masculine' political context a dramatic innovation in women-authored fiction, but Emecheta's heroine, Debbie Ogedemgbe is perhaps the apotheosis of the African New Woman. Certainly she is the most liberated and militant. When the novel opens Debbie has just returned from Britain where she took a degree at Oxford. Along with her closest friend, Babs Teteku, she is determined, despite her parents' objections, to join the army, an overwhelmingly male-dominated profession of course. And to emphasize the radicalism of Debbie's career choice, Emecheta dwells – perhaps rather heavy-handedly – on the fact that Debbie carries and sometimes brandishes that most obvious of all phallic symbols, a gun. From the very beginning we are left in no doubt over Debbie's feminism; neither marriage nor motherhood is a tenable option for her:

> If her parents thought they could advertise her like a fatted cow, they had another think coming. She would never agree to a marriage like theirs, in which the two partners were never equal. Her father always called the tune. She did not hate him . . . she loved both her parents very much. It was just that she did not wish to live a version of their life – to marry a wealthy Nigerian, ride the most expensive cars in the world, be attended by servants. No, she did not want that; her own ideas of independence . . . had no place in that set-up. She wanted to do something more than child breeding and rearing and being a good passive wife to a man whose ego she must boost all her days, while making sure to submerge every impulse that made her a full human being. (p. 45)

What Debbie does, in fact, is undertake a mission from the Nigerian government to travel to Biafra and try to persuade the Ojukwu-type Biafran leader, Abosi, to end the war. Lest we think, however, that Debbie is singled out for this difficult task because of her superior diplomatic skills, the entire mission is shot full of brutal reminders that as a Nigerian woman she is first, and above all, a sex object and prey to the lust of men. She is chosen to negotiate with Abosi solely because he had been in love with her before she became involved with her current lover, a whiteman,

Alan Grey. In other words, she is sent literally to seduce Abosi into surrendering. Sexual bargaining writ large, in short, and not all that different from the shrewd prostitution the heroines of *One is Enough* and *Double Yoke* practise, though it is true that Debbie is supposed to engage in this manipulation for the good of her country rather than her own self-interest. Then on her harrowing journey through Biafra to Abosi, Debbie is raped twice, by Nigerian and Biafran soldiers. The implications are painfully clear: the enemy is not Biafra or Nigeria or even the colonialists like Debbie's lover. The enemy is men, of any colour, any political persuasion.

Debbie is an unabashed feminist, but she is so completely Europeanized that one may ask whether she is also still an African woman. Like Adah Obi, the heroine of Emecheta's first two novels set in England, Debbie wants to be a writer and, indeed, during the course of the novel is writing her own account of the war entitled *Destination Biafra*. She is also revolutionary in her attitude toward her own sexuality, for in her liaison with Alan Grey she neither submits obediently nor attempts to gain rewards for her sexual acquiescence. Instead, like many Western women, she seeks her own sexual satisfaction and pleasure above all. And this is why her sexual victimization in Biafra is so shattering to her.

A telling scene which further calls into question Debbie's African identity occurs when she is fleeing through Biafra with a group of refugee Igbo women and children. She offers to help with one of the toddlers but has great difficulty getting the child securely tied on her back so that a watching soldier mocks her and asks:

> 'What type of women is Africa producing? This one can't even back a baby. How will you carry your own child when you have one?' . . . Debbie made light of it. But as she walked that dry road in the heat, with the weight of the child almost breaking her back, it struck her that African women of her age carried babies like this all day and still farmed and cooked; all she had to do now was walk, yet she was in such pain. What kind of African woman was she, indeed?' (p. 191)

But in the closing pages of the novel Debbie overcomes her doubts about her authenticity as an African woman. Indeed, when she rejects her white lover (the son of a former governor-general of Nigeria) she fuses her feminism with her anti-imperialist ideology: Alan Grey and his European culture, she asserts, are the ultimate patriarchal oppressors in Africa. She fails to blow up the South African plane Abosi is escaping from war-ravaged Biafra in, but she succeeds in defiantly repudiating Grey, also on the verge of flight, but eager for Debbie to leave with and marry him in Britain:

> I see now that Abosi and his like are still colonized. They need to be decolonized. I am not like him, a black white man; I am a woman and a woman of Africa. I am a daughter of Nigeria and if she is in shame, I shall stay and mourn with her in shame. No I am not ready yet to become the wife of an exploiter of my nation . . . Goodbye, Alan. I didn't mind your being my male concubine, but Africa will never again stoop to being your wife; to meet you on an equal basis, like companions, yes, but never again to be your slave. (pp. 258-9)

Debbie transmutes the personal into the political and asserts that her affair with Grey was a kind of allegory of the imperialistic rape of her country. It is a rousing speech to be sure; one can almost hear the ranks of feminist critics shouting bravo from the sidelines. But after the cheering has died down we have to concede that there is a contrived quality not merely to this closing scene but to the characterization of Debbie throughout the book. She is Emecheta's favourite heroine, perhaps because Debbie most transparently enacts her creator's political convictions. Certainly we can see Emecheta pulling the strings as Debbie tosses a grenade at Abosi's departing plane and hear Emecheta's refracted voice as Debbie triumphantly rejects Alan Grey. Debbie unfortunately is a flat, unchanging figure – something even of a puppet at times – in contrast to Ramatoulaye, Amaka, and figures from Emecheta's other novels like Ojebeta in *The Slave Girl* and Nnu Ego in *The Joys of Motherhood*. Debbie does not grow or develop. There is no depth or complexity in her characterization because she merely personifies an ideology, with the result that her behaviour is consistently static and predictable.

The problem Debbie poses to the reader and critic is related to the larger issue of evaluative criteria. How are we to judge a work which we find politically admirable and true but aesthetically simplistic, empty, or boring? What do we make of characters whose credos and pronouncements we endorse but whose human reality we find negligible? We are confronting here the vexed issue of commitment. Because so much of African literature is firmly rooted in social and political struggles and because most African writers – women as well as men – embrace a moral function for their work, it seems inappropriate, even pointless, to invoke 'pure' aesthetic standards by which to judge their writing. Critical dicta such as Henry James's 'give the artist his donne' and all a work of imagination need do is 'please' appear irresponsible in the context of African literature. Instead, we have, for example, Ngugi's and Micere Mugo's prescriptive Marxist standards of literary criticism. And the Nigerian feminist critic Molara Ogundipe-Leslie's asserts that 'the female writer should be committed in three ways: as a writer, as a woman, and as a Third World person; and her biological womanhood is implicated in all three.'[15]

Ogundipe-Leslie's deceptively simple but valid formulation is helpful when approaching works which stir our convictions but not our imaginations. And perhaps it is significant that she puts the requirement of _writer first._ If the writing is inferior the book becomes a tract and there are far more efficient and effective ways of spreading an ideology than by novels, especially in Third World countries where the literacy rate is often low. And it is also significant that Ogundipe-Leslie insists that a writer's 'womanhood is implicated in all three'; that it is inextricably bound up with all the other characteristics of a particular work. Women writers write first and foremost *as women.* From this perspective the most fundamental identity we possess is that of gender; all other determinants of selfhood – race, ethnic group, nationality – are imposed upon this primary sexual identity. Thus for a feminist critic, studying literature solely by genre, historical period or nationality is inadequate, even misleading. This is the point of Elaine Showalter's caveat that:

> 'insofar as our concepts of literary periodization are based on men's writing, women's writing must be forcibly assimilated to an irrelevant grid; we discuss a Renaissance which is not a renaissance for women, a Romantic period in which women played very little part, a modernism with which women conflict. At the same time, the ongoing history of women's writing has been suppressed, leaving large and mysterious gaps in accounts of the development of genre.[16]

And so, to return to *Destination Biafra*, we can say that though Emecheta's heart is in the right place, the book as a whole languishes in a shadowy region between manifesto and fiction. But if it lacks the resonance, lyricism, and complexity of such earlier Emecheta novels as *The Bride Price* and *The Slave Girl*, *Destination Biafra* at the very least possesses an historical importance in the development of African writing by women. It is the most forthright feminist novel to date; it steps beyond the confines of domestic life to imagine the role women have to play in the political struggles of their countries and, finally, whatever her flaws as a fictional creation, Debbie Ogedemgbe is the most compelling example we have of the New Woman in Africa. She embodies a liberating ideal of potentiality, of a rich, active, and fulfilling future for African women, and it is an autonomous future she embraces, a future without men.

In contrast to the aesthetic unevenness of *Destination Biafra*, Ama Ata Aidoo's *Our Sister Killjoy* is a stunning novel, an adroit, moving pastiche of interwoven fragments of poetry, dialogue, internal monologue, political fulminations (sometimes in verse), reverie, haunting descriptions and a long aching love letter which is never sent. And at the heart of this rich literary stew and binding all its ingredients together, is the figure of Sissie, Our Sister Killjoy.

Why Sissie and why Killjoy? 'Sissie' is short for Sister, a generic feminist appellation, as in Sisterhood. Sissie or Our Sister is also clearly intended by Aidoo to function as a representative figure. She is an African Everywoman, and the novel charts her solitary odyssey towards freedom. 'Killjoy' underlines her essential isolation. Sissie spurns all the easy lures that would compromise her integrity; however reluctantly, she rejects both lesbian and heterosexual love and also the comfortable, prosperous existence of exile in London. Most importantly, Sissie keeps faith with herself as a woman *and* an African. She succeeds in embracing both identities in a way that Debbie Ogedemgbe's rhetoric only vaguely adumbrates. Though both are intelligent, university-educated young women, Debbie is a sketchy stereotype of the African New Woman while Sissie is the flesh-and-blood real thing.

The novel is divided into four parts, each a particular phase in the journey of Sissie's self-discovery, a journey of departure and return. The form of the novel describes a circle as it follows Sissie's course from Africa to a students' summer programme in Germany to England and back to Africa. It is probably not coincidental that Sissie's progress reverses the European male exploration saga of the nineteenth century, the journey of discovery from Europe into the 'Dark Continent' and back to Europe again, 'a sadder and a wiser man'. Sissie's sojourns in Bavaria and London test and confirm her feminist consciousness, and her immersion in an alien culture strengthens her fidelity to her own.

The book begins and ends in flight, in transit between two worlds, Africa and Europe. When Sissie starts out she accepts the established view of Europe as a paradise of enlightenment and plenty: 'it was nearly dawn when they crossed the Mediterranean Sea. And as they left Africa, there was this other continent, lighted

up with the first streaks of glorious summer sunshine. Good night,
Africa. Good morning, Europe.'[17] But lest we take this naively
hopeful vision at Sissie's face value, Aidoo undercuts her heroine's
vision by entitling the first part of the novel 'Into a Bad Dream.'

In Bavaria Sissie is nearly lulled into a liaison with a young
German housewife who feeds her succulent plums and other
delicacies. It is an isolated, sensual female world the two women
share. Marija's husband works long shifts at a factory; her baby
sleeps from one nap to the next. Despite the fact that Sissie speaks
no German and Marija no English, the two women manage to establish a kind of hypnotic intimacy. But when Marija finally makes her
desire for Sissie obvious, Sissie recoils, more perhaps from the
European values Marija represents than from the sexuality of the
woman herself. Indeed, Sissie had fantasized being Marija's lover,
or rather had thought how nice it would have been if she were a
man. But the language barrier – in a metaphorical as well as literal
sense – proves insuperable. Sissie and Marija can 'touch' each
other as women, but the national and, even more importantly, the
racial gulf between them is unbreachable. Sissie boards a train
bound for Britain, clutching a paper bag from Marija full of liver
sausage, cheese, pastries, and plums.

In London Sissie is far more isolated than she was in Germany
because she finds herself more alienated from the male Ghanaian
students she meets there than she had been from Marija. Again we
see the primacy of gender over race or nationality. These young
Ghanaians are 'been-tos' with no intention of going back home. They
are hedonistic, deracinated, self-deceived, and it is Sissie's bad luck
to fall helplessly in love with one of them. She tries to persuade him to
go home, to give up the exile's irresponsible life in London, to return
where they belong and build up their country rather than endlessly
dissecting its woes from Britain. To no avail, of course.

The fourth part of the novel consists of Sissie's wrenching love
letter to this nameless young man – a record of her struggle
between her desire for him and her need to be true to herself and
the terrible isolation wrought by her heartbreaking victory when
the relationship ends. To everyone else, indeed even to herself in
her worst moments, her choice seems incomprehensible:

> If there is anyone I may have sinned against, it is me. That desiring you
> as I do, needing you as I do, I still let you go . . . all sorts of well-wishers
> have told me what I should have done in the first place . . . They say that
> any female in my position would have thrown away everything to be

with you, and remain with you: first her opinions, and then her own plans . . . What did I rather do but daily and loudly criticise you and your friends for wanting to stay forever in alien places? (p. 117)

However great her need and love, Sissie cannot give her 'lost heart', as she calls him, the obedience African men expect of women, and she, in fact, traces such female subordination to the imposition of European values: 'My Darling: it seems as if so much of the softness and meekness you and all the brothers expect of me and all the sisters is . . . really western.' And she goes on to contrast the strong, resourceful traditional African women to the 'dolls the colonisers brought along with them who fainted at the sight of their own bleeding fingers and carried smelling salts around all the time.' (p. 117). When Sissie returns to Ghana, then, she is returning to a culture she feels in its purest, uncontaminated form affords dignity and self-worth to women. Instead of seeing her African and feminist identities as incompatible, she maintains that one is conditional upon the other.

But Aidoo, unlike Emecheta, does not bestow an easy victory on her heroine. Far from defiantly rejecting her lover as Debbie does, Sissie suffers incalculable anguish over losing him:

'I just sat in my room and suffered. I didn't go mad as I feared, Allah is truly great. Something else happened though. Loneliness became my room-mate and took the place over . . . these cold countries are no places for anyone to be by themselves . . . There is a kind of loneliness overseas which is truly bad. It comes with the cold wind blowing outside the window making the trees moan so. It is there in the artificial heat in the room which dried my skin and filled my sleep with nightmares . . . My lost Heart, loneliness pursued me . . .' (p. 119)

Sissie writes this long, powerful 'Love Letter' on a flight back to Africa, and even before she lands she knows she will never post it. The love letter, in fact, has really been to herself, as was Ramatoulaye's 'so long a letter'; a 'cri de coeur', an apologia or confession, an act of self-scrutiny leading to self-awareness and finally self-validation. And this revelation and resolution wrought by the letter is completed just as Africa comes into view below Sissie:

Sure enough, there was Africa, huge and from this coastline, certainly warm and green. . . . Suddenly, she knew what she was not going to do. She was never going to post the letter . . . There was no need to mail it . . . Besides, she was back in Africa. And that felt like fresh honey on the tongue: a mixture of complete sweetness and smoky roughage. Below was home with its unavoidable warmth . . . Oh Africa. Crazy old continent. (p. 133)

Heat, colour, growth, renewal – in short, life – are what await Sissie as she touches down home. Her geographical voyage has mirrored a parallel internal one. Like Ramatoulaye, she has suffered, despaired, wept, but ultimately emerged whole: an African woman.

It is striking how many of these novels leave their heroines on the brink of autonomous, self-determining lives without men. Without a few exceptions like *One is Enough*, the feminist literary imagination in Africa has yet to delineate fully the new life of the African New Woman. To date there is no African *Golden Notebook* or *The Women's Room*. Instead, the focus has been on the necessary preliminary struggle – the radical repudiation of prevailing patriarchal roles and norms – perhaps because the subsequent reality of a creative life without men has been far from easy for most of these writers. The Egyptian feminist writer Nawal El Saadawi, for one, has written feelingly of the envy, hatred and ostracism that creative women in Africa provoke.[18] And Aidoo herself, who imagines Sissie integrating her African and feminist identities, has spoken with candour and bitterness about her experience as a woman writer and university lecturer in Ghana:

As an academic today, I wonder how I can maintain a vibrant intellect condemned as I am to ostracism only because I refuse to consider marriage as the only way to live. [Even in the university environment] no one expects a woman to perform well in any other areas apart from cooking, sewing, and other so-called traditional feminine activities . . . Once in a while . . . I catch myself wondering whether I would have found the courage to write if I had not started to write when I was too young to know what was good for me. Most certainly, my trials as a woman writer are heavier and much more painful than any I have to go through as a university teacher.[19]

Perhaps there is an answer in the above to the question of why Aidoo has produced so little writing in the twenty years since she wrote *The Dilemma of a Ghost* while she was still an undergraduate at the University of Ghana. Emecheta has bluntly said that she could not have written all her novels if she had stayed in Nigeria.[20] Life in Britain is far more conducive to women's creativity than West Africa is.

Most surprising is the fact that Emecheta and Nwapa actually deny that they are feminists at all, flying in the face of the patently clear orientation of their fiction. Molara Ogundipe-Leslie ascribes such denial 'to the successful intimidation of African women by men . . . Male ridicule, aggression and backlash have resulted in making women apologetic and have given the term "feminist" a bad name. Yet, nothing could be more feminist than the writings of these women writers in their concern for and deep understanding of the experiences and fates of women in society.'[21] It seems a matter with Emecheta and Nwapa of 'believe what I do not what I say' or, to reverse the old adage, they practise what they don't preach. But this very contradiction between their personal statements and their published work indicates the difficulty and self-division they suffer as African women writers.

Nevertheless, it is to the fiction that we must continue to turn. Imagined worlds are more potent than real ones, refined as they are of hesitation, doubt and compromise. All these novels speak of female solidarity, power, independence; of the liberation of women's bodies, minds, and spirits. They reconcile feminist aspiration and African integrity: they bestow wholeness, and call for rebirth and renewal. And if these things do not yet exist, these writers dream of a time when they shall, and we should be grateful for the power, beauty, and enduring truth of their vision.

NOTES

1. Kenneth Little, *The Sociology of Urban Women's Image in African Literature*, London, Macmillan, 1980.
2. Lloyd W. Brown, *Women Writers in Black Africa*, Westwood, Conn., Greenwood Press, 1981, p. 6.
3. Enid Schildkrout, 'Dependence and Autonomy: The Economic Activities of Secluded Hausa Women in Kano', in Christine Oppong (ed.), *Female and Male in West Africa*, London, Allen & Unwin, 1983, pp. 107–26.
4. Carmel Dinan, 'Sugar Daddies and Gold-Diggers: the White-Collar Single Woman in Accra', in Oppong (ed.), *Female and Male in West Africa*, pp. 344–66.
5. Quoted in ibid., p. 363.
6. Maria Rosa Cutrefelli, *Women of Africa: Roots of Oppression*, London, Zed Press, 1983, p. 3.

7. Beatrice Stegeman, 'The Divorce Dilemma: The New Woman in Contemporary African Novels', *Critique: Studies in Modern Fiction*, 15, no. 3, 1974, p. 90.

8. ibid., p. 92.

9. Charlotte H. Bruner (ed.), *Unwinding Threads: Writing by Women in Africa*, London, Heinemann, 1983, p. xiv.

10. Mariama Bâ, *So Long a Letter*, London, Virago Press, 1982, p. 72. Subsequent page references are to this edition and will be given in the text.

11. Flora Nwapa, *One is Enough*, Enugu, Nigeria, Tana Press, 1981, p. 23. Subsequent page references are to this edition and will be given in the text.

12. Interview with Katherine Frank, Freetown, Sierra Leone, January 1983.

13. Buchi Emecheta, *Double Yoke*, London, Ogwugwu Afor, 1982, p. 94. Subsequent page references are to this edition and will be given in the text.

14. Buchi Emecheta, *Destination Biafra*, London, Fontana, 1983, p. viii. Subsequent page references are to this edition and will be given in the text.

15. See p. 10 above. An earlier version of Ogundipe-Leslie's article appeared in *The Guardian* (Lagos), 21 December 1983.

16. Elaine Showalter, 'Feminist Criticism in the Wilderness', in Elizabeth Abel (ed.), *Writing and Sexual Difference*, Brighton, Harvester Press, 1982, p. 33.

17. Ama Ata Aidoo, *Our Sister Killjoy*, London, Longman, 1981, p. 11. Subsequent page references are to this edition and will be given in the text.

18. In Torill Stokland, Mallica Vajrathon and Davidson Nicol (eds), *Creative Women in Changing Societies: A Quest for Alternatives*, New York, Transnational Publishers, 1982, pp. 90–3.

19. ibid, pp. 69–71.

20. Interview with Katherine Frank, London, 10 February, 1984.

21. see above, p. 11.

Women in African Literature Today, E. D. Jones ed,
Trenton: Africa World Press 1987

Mother Africa on a Pedestal: The Male Heritage in African Literature and Criticism

Mineke Schipper

'Women have no mouth' (Beti proverb, Cameroon)

The physical differences between the sexes that children are born with have enormous effects on their entire lives. In any given cultural context, male and famale behaviour patterns are fixed by norms, and anyone who tries to break the rules can expect to meet with serious problems in a community in which the ruling group produces images and conceptions of the others to legitimise the status quo.[1]

A recent UN study of women's position in the world showed that women do two-thirds of all the work both within and outside the home. But they only receive 10 per cent of all the money earned on earth. And they possess less than a hundredth of all the wealth of the world.

In Africa, illiteracy is four times more prevalent among women than among men and in the schools the proportion of girls falls as the level of education rises. In this context, it is not surprising to see that most African literature has been written by men, and that most critics of African literature are men as well.

I do not believe that we should re-open here the discussion whether the 'other' is at all capable of studying or writing about 'us'. This discussion took place in the context of the obvious *Eurocentrism* which for a long time determined the perspective of so many Western (and even a number of African) scholars – the 'other' being the European, 'us' being the Africans.[2]

Nowadays, the same question is obviously of current interest among feminist critics: the radicals reject the male perspective once and for all, as belonging to the 'other' and therefore inadequate to study 'us' or 'our texts' for that matter, particularly because of the unsurmountable *viricentrism* in literary texts as well as in literary criticism. However, openness and awareness are a better research guide than narrow-minded protectionist prescriptions.

I believe the starting point should be that every subject can be dealt with by any writer or critic, and that only the result is to be examined carefully. Therefore, the first question is logically: what do the texts say?

In the oral tradition, we often do not even know whether the storyteller who thought up a particular story was a man or a woman. Of course when one examines the recorded texts, one might wonder whether a myth or story doesn't serve particular interests in a given society.

As far as written literature is concerned, we know that the main bulk of texts has been written since colonial times. This has certainly affected the depiction of women in colonial as well as in African literature. The fact that most African literature and criticism up till now has been produced by male authors quite naturally leads to the question as to whether this very fact *has* made any difference. Has the 'male heritage' influenced African literature? If so, how and to what extent?

In the following pages, I shall examine three factors that have contributed in different ways to the development of woman's image in African literature. These are (1) the mythological 'prephase'; (2) the colonial heritage; and (3) developments since the 1960s.

We shall try to relate these points by comparing the images produced in their respective (con)texts. As always in literary history, the African woman today is creating her own literary texts on the basis of inherited literary and social conditions, on the one hand continuing existing traditions and on the other hand opposing them. We shall conclude with some reflections on the critic's attitude toward the woman writer.

Beyola witch

The Mythological 'Pre-phase'

In the story of Genesis in the Bible, we are told in detail about the creation of man. He is the first human being; woman comes later, she originates from man and is therefore part of him, relegated to a secondary position. Many passages in the Bible confirm the supremacy of man over woman – or at least that is how they have been interpreted. Patriarchal patterns of culture are also to be found in Islam. The Qur'an says: 'Men are the managers of the affairs of women for that Allah has preferred in bounty one of them over the other'. (Sura 4: 34) Studies on women's position in Africa make it clear that the replacement of traditional ideas by Western ones has not proved to be a guarantee for the amelioration of women's position. On the contrary, they may have only served to strengthen ideas which many African creation and origin myths already contained.[3]

Myths are supposed to contain the truth, and the dogmas and utterances in them are not to be doubted in the community. Of course they have, in fact, very often been manipulated and adapted according to the interests of the people in power. Myths explain and justify how man created order from chaos and how, by way of culture, he imposed his will on nature. In myth, woman has been associated (by man?) with nature in two main senses, one positive and the other negative: as the life-giving mother figure and as the frightening, dangerous witch who has to be dominated or at least restricted by codes and norms. A number of myths explain how the existing hierarchical order was created and how it has been ever since – from the beginning. Looking at African creation myths woman, in comparison with man, has often had to put up with a secondary position.

There is much more to say about woman in African creation myths than can be said in the limited context of an article. Here, we must confine ourselves to a few observations. In a Luba myth from Zaire, the Supreme Being, Kabezya Mpungu, created two people, a man and a woman who had no soul or *mutima* yet. It was only after God left the earth that he sent *mutima* 'in a little vase the size of a hand'. *Mutima* entered the first man but nothing is said about the soul of the first woman. It reminds one of the European discussions among medieval philosophers about whether woman had a soul at all.

Very often, woman is mythologically discriminated against. When man and woman did not originate at the same time, the woman was almost never created first. More than once, she came into being accidentally, as in the following Saramo myth (Tanzania):

> Long ago there were no women. There were only two men who lived on honey. One of the men climbed into a tree. There was honey inside the tree and he wanted to get it out with his axe. The sharp blade of the axe fell down and hit the other man, who was lying on his back asleep. The axe fell onto his penis and cut it off. What was left was a bleeding wound, like women have.
> His companion climbed down and asked:
> 'What is that?'
> 'The axe cut it off,' he replied.
> Then they slept together and a girl was born. They slept together again and a boy was born. A world of people descended from those two men. Ever since that day, women lose blood, just like that first woman did. (p. 103).

Here woman is a mutilated man. A Fang myth(Gabon) has man created by God, whereas woman is made by man from a piece of wood. In another Fang myth, woman originated from one of man's toes.[4]

The Asante (Ghana) explain how man and woman came together against the will of the creator. It is clearly emphasized that man not woman committed the first transgression; he made his way into the woman's camp. Nevertheless, woman is punished much more severely than man:

> Here is the punishment for the men: when a man sees a woman whom his heart desires he will have to give her gold, clothes and many other fine things before he can possess her. And here is the punishment for the women: since you also disobeyed, when you see a man whom your heart desires you will have to keep it to yourself in your head! In addition, you will have to pound the fufu and do all the work, before eating it yourself . . . You will be with child nine to ten months and you shall give birth in great pain. (pp. 101f)

When it comes to original sin or the Fall which destroys the paradise situation, it is woman's doing in most cases. Among the Tutsi (Rwanda), for instance, woman let her tongue run away with her and betrayed the secret of Imana, the Supreme Being; whereupon her children were driven out of heaven. In the Hungwe myth (Zimbabwe), it was Morongo who seduced her husband so that he made love to her against the will of the God Moari. Bambara mythology blames the first woman Muso Kuroni for destroying the original harmony. The Kulwe(Tanzania) creation myth blames the fact that people have to work and that they know hunger and perdition on the woman who did not respect God's command to grind only one grain of wheat (which would then multiply), and thus ruined the earth (pp. 88f). The same happened in the Bini myth (Nigeria) where men did not have to till the ground because they could cut off a piece of the sky and eat it whenever they felt hungry. The sky warned them not to cut off too much because he did not want to be thrown on the rubbish heap. And then it was again 'a greedy woman' who cut off an exorbitant piece of the sky which neither she nor anybody could finish. The remainder was thrown on the rubbish heap and 'the sky became very angry indeed, and rose up high above the earth, far beyond the reach of men. And from then on men have had to work for their living.'[5] There are many more examples, but the ones cited above, from different parts of Africa, illustrate the degree to which woman was blamed for what went wrong.

Fortunately, there are a few rare exceptions to the anti-female rule found in so many myths. A myth of the Ekoi in Nigeria says that at the beginning of time, only women populated the earth. By mistake Obassi (God) himself killed one of these sisters. To make up for his mistake, he offered to give them anything they wanted of all his possessions. One by one, the women refused all the things Obassi mentioned. At the end, only one thing remained on the list: man.

> They took man, therefore, as compensation for the fellow woman who they had lost. Thus men became the servants of women, and have to work for them to this day. For, though a woman comes under the influence of her husband upon marriage, yet she is his proprietor, and has a right to ask any service, and to expect him to do whatever she chooses. (p. 104)

However, Obassi Nsi, the God here, must have originally been a goddess (the earth goddess?), as the informant explained to P.A. Talbot who noted this myth in 1912: 'Obassi Nsi must be a woman and our mother, because everybody knows that mothers have the tenderest heart'.[6] Nonetheless, Obassi Nsi has since become a male God, although the myth is still told in this pro-female form.

Why have women so often – and not only in African mythology – been blamed for all the wrong in the world? In fact we do not know where anti-female mythical literature comes from, but myths survived at the roots of what society gradually became. Not only in myths, but also in fairy tales and all sorts of other stories, woman may be depicted as a dangerous force, as threatening nature, a witch, a negative power, as the one who swallows or castrates man, as Denise Paulme showed in her *La mère dévorante*.[7]

In the same or in other stories, besides the image of woman as a negative force, we find the opposite view, woman as the tender virgin or the virtuous maternal character. The positive view of woman is usually associated with her reproductive function, the dearly loved and loving mother who takes care of her children and sacrifices herself for them. Both views are widely prevalent in African oral literature.

The Colonial Heritage

In her well-known book *Le deuxième sexe*, Simone de Beauvoir – and with her many others in the Western world who stand up for the rights of the (Western?) woman – sees obvious parallels between the situation of women and blacks. According to her, both groups are struggling to get rid of the same paternalistic grip of the white man that wants to keep them in their proper place, i.e. the place he has destined for them. The white man, she says, speaks highly of the qualities of the good black, who is child-like, unaware of his situation, easily amused and resigned to his lot. In much the same way, he appreciates the woman who is really a woman, puerile, irresponsible, vain, the woman who recognizes man's superiority and who is pleased to submit to him.[8]

In an interview with the Senegalese poet and former head of state, Léopold Sédar Senghor in 1974, I asked for his comment on these ideas of Simone de Beauvoir in *Le deuxième sexe*. Senghor agreed completely; according to him, women and blacks are so much more emotional than the 'hard-hearted man who tyrannizes them'. The question, then, is what does the African woman become in this field of force; twice oppressed, by the white man and by the black brother?

This kind of comparison between the situations of (white) women and blacks in the world has been made in Western feminist circles and sometimes still is, but it is not current at all in Africa (the case of Senghor is quite exceptional and his negritude theories about 'raison hellène' and 'émotion nègre' are well-known). Who has ever seen a black man expressing his sincere compassion for the tragic fate of the poor oppressed white woman? It is certainly not evident in African novels written by men. One would search in vain for black characters who are aware of being victims together with the Western woman of white man's stranglehold of discrimination. On the contrary! In the eyes of the colonized African, the white woman is a privileged being par excellence, as she has no reason to complain about her position, as many novels show. For instance, Margery Thompson in Ngugi's *A Grain of Wheat* led a life of luxury with nothing to do but give orders to her servants.[9] In the colonial situation, a woman who would have been an insignificant person in Europe, doing her own housekeeping and taking care of her own children, is granted unprecedented opportunities to exercise power over one or more subordinates. Power which is too easily misused, as the African novels about the colonial period show. From the African point of view, the white woman is indeed a serious racist factor in colonial society as the South African situation still clearly illustrates.[10]

In the novels – especially in the francophone ones – on the other hand, a lot of attention is devoted to the looks of the white woman, her white skin, the colour of her eyes and her hair, her hairstyle, her clothes, her make-up. Often it is said that she is beautiful and well dressed; blue eyes and fair hair are obviously preferred. The more out of reach she seems, the more she is idealized. In Ferdinand Oyono's *Une vie de boy*, for instance, Toundi praises the beauty of his Madame, the wife of the French Commandant. She has just arrived from Europe and is not yet aware of the colonial mentality which she is soon to adopt. So she shakes hands with him, an unusual gesture in colonial society. Toundi writes about her in his diary:

> My happiness has neither day nor night . . . I have held the hand of my queen. I felt that I was really alive. From now on my hand is sacred and must not know the lower regions of my body. My hand belongs to my queen whose hair is the colour of ebony, with eyes that are like the antelope's, whose skin is pink and white as ivory. A shudder ran through my body at the touch of her tiny moist hand. She trembled like a flower dancing in the breeze. My life was mingling with hers at the touch of her hand. Her smile is refreshing as a spring of water. Her look is as warm as a ray from the setting sun. It bathes you in a light that warms the depth of the heart. I am afraid . . . afraid of myself.[11]

In *Soul on Ice*, Eldridge Cleaver stated that, for oppressed blacks, the white woman is the symbol of freedom – a quite different view of the situation from Simone de Beauvoir's. Blacks, he says, dream of the white woman and put her on a pedestal; she is especially desirable because unlike himself and the black woman she is not submissive. This perspective explains Toundi's above-mentioned reaction in *Une vie de boy*.

In *Peau noire, masques blancs*, Frantz Fanon emphasizes that oppressed black people often seek to liberate themselves by choosing a woman with lighter skin: her love could make him less black; the whiter the freer. This liberation, he writes, would be best symbolized by the 'whitest woman, the blonde with the blue eyes'. According to Fanon, this kind of reasoning is based on norms of 'white superiority' which, of course, have been imposed by colonialism and by Western propaganda in films and magazines.[12]

In spite of her beauty, the white woman in the African novel is usually depicted as a moody and discontented creature. She rarely has a status of her own, she has no job and is completely dependent on her husband and his profession; she is only somebody's wife. She is usually preoccupied by her appearance, her beauty, her figure, her clothes and her jewellery. The other thing colonial Western women seem to be interested in as far as the novels are concerned is the topic of Africa and Africans, whom they talk about endlessly, usually in a negative way. There are endless complaints about the damned country, the miserable climate, the heat, the downpours that spoil the tennis courts, the fact that there is no decent hairdresser and so on; and then there are the Africans themselves, lazy liars and thieves. All this is brought forward as the way Western women think; these characters are bored, their marriages are a failure, they work off their bad temper on their staff, as Toundi's Madame does in Oyono's novel.[13]

Their lack of interest and imagination makes them capricious and unpredictable. In fact, these female characters in African novels correspond exactly with the description Simone de Beauvoir presents in *Le deuxième sexe* of the 'real feminine woman', the fatuous, frivolous little person we referred to earlier. The negative impression that the Western woman obviously made in Africa can be found in a wide range of novels. It is often even made worse by the racism and prejudice she arouses in herself and in other colonials in a society offering fertile grounds for these feelings. In short, the Western woman is depicted in African novels by male writers – especially those set in colonial times – as the dangerous, frivolous, adulterous type (European marriages are generally unhappy and infidelity is more of a rule than an exception). She is hardly ever presented as the positive, thoughtful caring mother.

African novelists have indeed devoted great effort to projecting a negative image of the Western woman, but they depict African girls and women who adopt aspects of 'modern' life no less critically. Often, little consideration is given to the fact that there may be positive advantages in turning away from certain traditions.

African women in the novels often see white women as dangerous rivals, so they do their best to imitate them in order to please their African boyfriends, or to find a European lover themselves. Following the examples of Western women, they also start wearing tight clothes, even trousers, which show off their figures. Older people find this shocking. Modern women try to straighten their hair; they use lipstick and often seem to prefer European languages to their own. The older generation (and the male writer) is worried about these developments, since the white women have always been the epitome of impudence and wickedness: morals and traditions are in danger of being lost if 'our' women identify with this example. Western glamour films have also contributed toward imposing the stereotypical image of the Western woman in Africa.[14] Consequently, the African woman who tries to Westernize her looks and who exhibits a certain independence is also stereotyped as not really to be trusted. She is often viewed as the antithesis of the traditional virtuous caring mother: again two camps according to the good–bad scheme. 'Modern' motherhood seems a contradiction in terms. Ekwensi's *Jagua Nana* is an example: she wears a low-cut transparent blouse 'through which her pink brassiere could be seen – provocatively – and much more besides'. Jagua – 'sheath dress, painted lips and glossy hair' – goes with her boyfriend Freddy to the Tropicana Club. This is how the women there are presented:

> All the women wore dresses which were definitely undersize, so that buttocks and breasts jutted grotesquely above the general contours of the bodies. At the same time the midriffs shrunk to suffocation. A dress succeeded if it made men's eyes ogle hungrily in this modern super sex-market.[15]

As we know, Jagua ends well: back in the village, she becomes a loving mother so that virtue triumphs over evil at the (happy) end.

One of the most famous examples of this opposition is Okot p'Bitek's *Song of Lawino*. Our sympathy is drawn towards Lawino and her complaints about the behaviour of her rival Clementine, who lightens her skin and tries to lose weight, 'like a white woman'. Thanks to her 'modern' features she impresses Lawino's husband Ocol, who has had a Western education and is now trying to get rid of his traditional wife. Clementine wants to look like a white woman, since she believes that this will make her beautiful, but from the traditional point of view she is not. On the contrary, 'modern' behaviour is considered 'shameless'. The Clementines dance like white people dance, held tightly; they kiss like white people do and the Lawinos are shocked:

> I am completely ignorant
> Of the dances of foreigners
> And I do not like it.
> Holding each other
> Tightly, tightly,
> In public,
> I cannot.
> I am ashamed.
> Dancing without a song
> Dancing silently like wizards,
> Without respect, drunk . . .
>
> If someone tries
> To force me to dance this dance
> I feel like hanging myself
> Feet first![16]

In the 1960s, Okot p'Bitek idealized the African tradition just as much as the négritude poets did in the 1930s. The idealization of the past was used to emphasize African dignity in the face of Western colonial domination, which threatened to destroy the traditional culture. At the same time, however, this romantic nostalgia that the African writer seems to cherish with respect to the female traditional role is not very conducive to women's emancipation, especially if she has no choice but the one between being a Lawino or a Clementine. Unfortunately, from the male writer's perspective, there seems to be hardly any other choice for her. Modern African women risk being accused of losing their African identity, a reproach (which one can hardly defend oneself against) much less heard in the case of men.

Since the 1960s: A New Perspective?

In her interesting book *Emancipation féminine et roman africain*, Arlette Chemain-Degrange carefully analysed the image of the woman in the francophone African novel. Significantly, up till

1975, all of these novels in French had been written by male writers.[17] She arrived at the conclusion that, in general, male writers simply take it for granted that woman submits to man and to tradition. Of course it is true that women played a role of their own in traditional African society, but men did too, and today they do not want to go back to the past. Doesn't an African proverb say that the river never returns to its source? In the novels, however, a woman who shows her independence is often punished for it.

However there are male novelists who advocate African women's liberation and do not adhere to the stereotypes of good (= the traditional loving mother) and bad (= the modern, evil, vicious girl). Sembène Ousmane is a significant example of emancipated thinking: he mercilessly highlights women's inequality and criticizes their resignation to their fate. He also shows the role that women should play in the development of society, for instance in political actions such as the railway strike in *God's Bits of Wood*. There are many other writers who broach the dilemma of liberation versus conservatism, but it is more often in a moderate, if not conservative, rather than a radical way, from the woman's point of view.

Gaining equal rights is obviously a wearisome task, not only because of the power of parental authority but also because of the fact that most men comfortably prefer to preserve discrimination when it suits their purpose. If women point this out, they are accused of having been influenced by Western women's liberation movements and that is the end of that. Francis Imbuga's play, *The Married Bachelor* shows both points of view. Mary lives with her boyfriend Denis. When she tells him that she already has a child by someone else he kicks her out, even though he himself has a son by another woman. Aren't they in the same situation? Denis does not think so:

DENIS: You are a woman. I am a man. You have once been pregnant. I have not. Do you still believe us to be similar?
MARY: But the basic facts are the same.
DENIS: Basic facts? What do you know about basic facts. The trouble with women is that you listen to the preaching of some western intellectual, talking about the equality of men and women and you imagine he is right. What you fail to realize is that woman is dangerously handicapped. This calls for more restriction of her physical desires. Women must exercise greater control over themselves if they are to retain their dignity in society. Right now yours, if you had any, has vanished into thin air.
MARY: Please, Denis, be kind. You are hurting me. Please.

DENIS: I am not hurting you. You hurt yourself the moment you allowed a man to share a blanket with you, give you a child and get away with it.[18]

Why should men be more equal than women? It has to do with society's heritage of traditions and norms. Men often want for themselves the same authority in their homes as their fathers had, an authority that was sanctioned by tradition and myths of the past. Young men want to marry virgins, and girls are given in marriage to husbands by fathers who do not have to ask their daughters' opinion. The women are expected to be faithful to their husbands, but have no right to ask the same in return. The men often have quite different norms, those that suit their male convenience.

In Buchi Emecheta's novel *Double Yoke*, a woman's point of view of virginity is presented with a great deal of irony. The female character Nko is rejected by her boy friend, because 'he was not sure that I was a virgin when we first made love'. Her friend Julia immediately wants to know whether Nko had asked him if he was a virgin too.[19]

Today, women writers are increasingly aware of their sisters' inequality in society and have started to write about it. Emecheta straightforwardly reveals her views of womanhood and of traditional society, which are much less idyllic than in the works of many a male writer before her; *The Joys of Motherhood* leaves no doubt about that.[20] She is one of the best known anglophone women writers in Africa. On the francophone side, the first woman writer who really attracted international attention was the Senegalese Mariama Bâ whose first novel *Une si longue lettre* had an enormous impact in her country as well as elsewhere.[21] In an interview at the end of the Dutch edition of her book, she says:

In all cultures, the woman who formulates her own claims or who protests against her situation is given the cold shoulder. If the woman who expresses herself orally is already labelled in a special way, the women who dare fix their thoughts for eternity are criticised all the more. Thus women are still hardly represented among African writers. And yet they have so much to say and write about . . . The woman writer in Africa has a special task. She has to present the position of women in Africa in all its aspects. There is still so much injustice. In spite of the fact that for a decade the United Nations have paid special attention to woman's problems, in spite of beautiful speeches and praiseworthy intentions, women continue to be discriminated. In the family, in the institutions, in society, in the street, in political organi-aions, discrimination reigns supreme. Social pressure shamelessly

suffocates individual attempts at change. The woman is heavily bur-
dened by mores and customs, in combination with mistaken and egoistic
interpretations of different religions . . . As women, we must work for
our own future, we must overthrow the status quo which harms us and
we must no longer submit to it. Like men, we must use literature as a
non-violent but effective weapon. We no longer accept the nostalgic
praise to the African Mother who, in his anxiety, man confuses with
Mother Africa. Within African literature, room must be made for
women . . ., room we will fight for with all our might.[22]

These words sound full of hope and strength. Unfortunately,
Mariama Bâ died at the age of fifty-two, a few months after this
interview.

In reality, male reactions to women's liberation efforts in
African society are often alarming, especially when the future of
the society as a whole seems critical or hopeless. Ngandu Nkashama
clearly emphasized this in an interesting article on contemporary
theatre in Zaire. As recently as 1982, he made the following comments about images of women:

Often she is considered to be the cause of all social misery, because of
her perfidy, her subtle playing with evil in all its forms, her use of
ambiguous language, her mean and narrow-minded spirit full of scan-
dals, luxury and lewdness . . . Woman's guilt is also attested to in her
abandoning of her primordial role which had made her the guardian of
tradition, protecting oracle of future societies. Carried along in the
dizzily violent circle of the new cities, with their deep loneliness and
their terrible fright, woman becomes the place in which the drama of
the whole people 'dis-occults itself'. [*se désocculte*][23]

Abortions, killings, suicides, adultery, these images of woman in
the theatre constitute, in fact, the trial of an (in)human community
adrift. Feminism, according to Ngandu, is associated, for example,
with traditional images of women grave-diggers, and societies of
witches who eat their own children etc. In this theatre in the 1980s,
one finds negative characters such as the 'sterile woman', who is
violently tortured; the 'fallen woman' and the 'incestuous girl' in
plays by Mambambu, Mususua and Ngenzhi Lonta.

All these plays stress the destruction of cultural identity: the
dislocated family, the towns that destroy human relationships,
social crises that reject people as such. Ngandu concludes that if
the man sets such great store by the image of woman, it is because
he has problems recognizing his own image in a society that rejects
him, if not debases him. To him, this is not anti-feminism but the
transposition of the whole social drama on the image of the woman

charged with the anger of a society unable to put its situation into words.[24]

This is all very well, but the question remains: why should the woman be the only scapegoat? Why should she once again be blamed for all the wrong in today's society? Is it because she is in a weaker position and therefore more a victim than he is? Or because the male perspective prevents him from blaming man – even partly? Ngandu's examples exphasize this and, moreover, there is no female playwright among the ones mentioned and quoted by him. It is even possible that there are still none at all in Zaire. In African literature as a whole woman hardly has a mouth yet. The image of women in the novel is also very much a male writer's business, and often sadly stereotyped, especially in the urban novel where she is mainly depicted negatively, as a source of perdition and of menace.

In an interview I had with Buchi Emecheta in Amsterdam in May 1983, she complained about the way in which male colleagues often presented their female characters: 'A writer like Cyprian Ekwensi, for example, has got brilliant daughters, so why should he put down the women in his novels the waý he does? I really do not understand'.

In a study of the image of woman in the Kenyan novel Eleanor Wachtel concludes that the 'modern' woman was continually associated with the evils of the city, such as drinking, violence, temptation and prostitution. She is depicted as a contemptuous parasite against the cherished background of the ideal traditional mother image. This easily leads to the stereotyped antitheses of mother–whore which, according to Eleanor Wachtel, are frequently found in contemporary Kenyan novels because they have been written by men:

> As in nearly all third-world countries, most of the Kenyan novelists are men. Their central characters are preponderantly males. Further, the male viewpoint is underlined not only by the many characterizations of young men, but by the literary device of the first person protagonist . . . This is quite natural to the relatively inexperienced author who would tend to be somewhat autobiographical anyway. At the same time, however, it is also more intimate, personal and hence, more explicitly male in outlook and tone . . . This device creates rapport between author and reader and enlists the latter's sympathy. It does not allow for another point of view . . . Women are necessarily 'the other'. In Kenya this male-focused lens on life is an accurate reflection of society. It is consistent with a society where men are the primary decision-makers.[25]

The only solution to this is the one to be implemented by women writers themselves: they must pick up their pens and express their own ideas about woman in African society, and thus correct or complement the one-sidedness of certain perspectives. This was indeed one of the conclusions of a number of women writers at a conference on African women and literature organized by the University of Mainz in 1982.[26] At this conference, the above-mentioned tendency to confuse Mother Africa with the African mother Mariama Bâ alluded to, was also emphasized by the South African novelist Miriam Tlali. As she put it, 'it is a problem when men want to call you Mother Africa and put you on a pedestal, because then they want you to stay there forever without asking your opinion – and unhappy you if you want to come down as an equal human being!' In the past women often accepted this, but they are less willing to do so in the contemporary urban context.

It is always difficult to start sharing power if one is used to being the master. For people who never had power, the changes can only be for the better. This has proved true in the past in the case of colonial domination, but the question is still who profited from this new power structure. Very few women did. Girls today receive less education and (as in the West) what they receive is more often of a domestic rather than of a technical nature.

At the Second International Book Fair of Radical Black and Third World Books in London in April 1983, it was obvious that a number of black men in Africa had already made an important impact in world-wide literary circles, whereas black women were still struggling for recognition and were just starting to express the feelings and experiences of their sisters 'silenced by tradition'. In the words of Jane Bryce: 'black women have extended the meaning of words like "colonisation" and "barbarism" to include the specific experience of women in both black and white societies'.[27]

Two critical attitudes

The field of criticism is still just as male-dominated as that of creative writing; this was clearly emphasized at the Mainz Conference. The present writer had to think of this, when looking for literary criticism and comments on the works of African women writers. In the main anthologies, essays on West African or East African women writers are hardly in evidence. It is true that there is now a book by Lloyd Brown on *Women Writers in Black Africa*.[28]

The question is whether dealing separately with women's literature does not lead to a covert way of keeping them 'out of the official circuit'. However that may be, more attention is being devoted, little by little, to African women writers, as is also evident from this special issue of *African Literature Today*.

As far as critics are concerned, I should like to emphasize here the difference between what I call *exclusive* and *inclusive* criticism. Exclusion has often been used for the purpose of subjugation: this was a well known policy of the colonial masters, who tended to exclude Africa from what they called civilization.

Generally, we can distinguish these two approaches in criticism. In the first one, the critic takes his own culture, history, ideology and so on, as a (consciously or unconsciously) preconceived model and examines every text from that particular point of view. The other approach is that of the open-minded critic who is not bent upon including or excluding texts according to his own current value system, but who reads literary texts within the contexts from which they originated. Of course, inclusive criticism demands more of the critic since nothing is fixed in advance, especially when texts by authors from other cultures or ideologies, or of the other sex are concerned. The critic should be very well aware of what he is talking about; he has to be erudite (and modest!) in a new world-wide sense, and not only be familiar with his own culture, history, value system and context, but also with the other's. The openness of the inclusive approach has the advantage that the critic has not been excessively influenced by standard Western or male (or both) dominated values. Of course this is not easy, especially for people who are not even aware of the existence of different value systems. African critics who have the experience of values being dictated by Eurocentric exclusive criticism may have a head start on Western critics, as they would have seen how objectionable exclusive criticism can be. Unfortunately there is no guarantee that this will be the case.

An attempt will be made to illustrate this point by giving an example of both sorts of criticism involving women writers. Femi Ojo-Ade reveals himself as an example of the exclusive critic, when he tells the African woman writer what to do or rather what not to do in his 'Female Writers, Male Critics':

> The [women] writers that we have studied dwell too much upon the malady of male chauvinism, a phenomenon that, in its most famous aspect, is no less a Western way than the notions of feminism espoused by some female writers. Blackness, Africanness . . . is almost foreign to

others who have let the questions of male domination blind them to the necessary solidarity between man and woman.[29]

At the Mainz Conference, the African women writers and critics rejected precisely this kind of viewpoint because they felt that it was unfair; it was also all too easy and simple to try to combat their striving for equality by saying that it was under Western womens' influence. The other well-known argument is of course that women lose their femininity, when they demand equal rights, as Ojo-Ade suggests indeed in his article on Mariama Bâ. According to this critic, 'as an expression of freedom' the feminism of Ramatoulaye, the heroine of the novel:

> constitutes only a partial aspect of the totality of African life. Femininity is the virtue of the traditionalist; feminism, the veneer of the progressive striving to become a man.[30]

Does femininity still equal submissiveness?

An example of an inclusive critic is Eustace Palmer, who, in an excellent article, looks without prejudice at Emecheta's *Joys of Motherhood*. Without balancing feminism against blackness, he appreciates with great care Emecheta's woman's perspective as a contribution to the whole of African literature and does not regard it (as Ojo-Ade does) as a 'deviant perspective':

> The picture of the cheerful contented female complacently accepting her lot is replaced by that of a woman who is powerfully aware of the unfairness of the system and who longs to be fulfilled in her self, to be a full human being, not merely somebody else's appendage.[31]

He is aware of the critic's problems that are to be expected in view of this new approach of a 'reality' which is not his own:

> What gives this novel its peculiar quality is the unashamed presentation of the woman's point of view. This comes out not merely in the powerful evocation of Nnu Ego's misery but even in the narrator's own omniscient comments . . . There will be many who will find Emecheta's analysis of the female situation controversial; her presentation may not be able to stand up to sociological scrutiny. But *The Joys of Motherhood* is an imaginative and not a scientific work, and the artist is surely within her rights to exaggerate or even to depart from sociological authenticity. The novel must be judged as a work of art and it is difficult to deny the accomplishment of the artistry.[32]

This broadness of the male critical mind is often lacking in the discussion of works by women. The main problem, however, is that men are not used to taking the female perspective into account, since it has so often been hidden or kept from men by the women themselves, because of personal interest or fear of reprisals, just as African views were kept from white colonizers by the Africans, in the past. Today, some women have the courage to reflect in the mirror of their writings their own views and experiences of the hierarchical role patterns, as well as the violation of the status quo by daring female characters.

One can like it or not, one can get angry and tell them 'to behave', but that would mean dictating one's perspective at the expense of someone else's, and denying that someone else the right to have and express any personal view on 'reality' at all.

Therefore I should like to remind the reader of an old statement by Chinua Achebe – which I alter slightly with his permission – because in this new context it has lost neither its deep wisdom nor its relevance:

> The *male* critic of African literature must cultivate the habit of humility appropriate to his limited experience of thé *female* world and purged of the superiority and arrogance which history so insidiously makes him heir to.[33]

Achebe used the word *European* in his text instead of 'male' and the word *African* instead of 'female': he was addressing the Eurocentric Western critic. He has also asserted that his statement, which dates from 1962, made him 'quite a few bitter enemies: one of them took my comments so badly – almost as a personal affront – that he launched numerous unprovoked attacks against me.[34] Are African critics any wiser today than European ones were twenty years ago?[35]

NOTES

1. See for instance Christine Obbo, *African Women: Their Struggle for Economic Independence*, London, Zed Press, 1981.
2. I.e. the methodological discussion of whether African literature

should be so different as to demand different methods to study it. See for instance the papers I edited for the African Studies Centre, *Text and Context in Africa: Methodological Explorations in the Field of Literature*, Leiden, African Studies Centre, 1977.

3. Unless stated otherwise, the creation myths referred to here are to be found in my collection *Het zwarte paradijs, Afrikaanse scheppings-mythen*, Massbree, Corrie Zelen, 1980. Page references to this book are inserted in the text. Unfortunately, this book which contains fifty creation myths (chosen among hundreds) from all over Africa, is not yet available in English.

4. ibid., pp. 19ff.

5. Ulli Beier (ed.), *The Origin of Life and Death*, London, Heinemann, 1974, p. 51.

6. P.A. Talbot, *In the Shadow of the Bush*, London, Heinemann, 1912, p. 17.

7. Denise Paulme, *La mère dévorante*, Paris, Gallimard, 1975.

8. Simone de Beauvoir, *Le deuxième sexe. I. Les faits et les mythes*, Paris, Gallimard, 1949, pp. 24-5.

9. Ngugi wa Thiong'o, *A Grain of Wheat*, London, Heinemann, (1967), 1976, p. 34.

10. See, for instance, Jacklyn Cock, *Maids and Madams. A Study in the Politics of Exploitation*, Johannesburg, Ravan Press, 1980. In my book *Le Blanc vu d'Afrique*, Amsterdam/Yaoundé 1973, I have analysed the francophone African novels on the subject of the image of the white man and the Western world up till 1966. One chapter deals with the Western woman, see pp. 135-168.

11. Ferdinand Oyono, *Une vie de boy*, Paris, Julliard, 1960. English translation, *Houseboy*, London, Heinemann, 1966, pp. 55-6.

12. Eldridge Cleaver, *Soul on Ice*, New York, McGraw-Hill, 1968. Frantz Fanon, *Peau noire, masques blancs*, Paris, Editions du Seuil, 1952.

13. See Oyono, *Vie de boy*.

14. Cf. *Le Blanc vu d'Afrique*, pp. 145ff. An example from the African novel in English is Margery Thompson's affair with Dr Van Dyke in Ngugi's *Grain of Wheat*. See also Alan Burns, *Le préjugé de race et de couleur*, Paris, Payot, 1949, p. 41: 'There is no doubt that passionate love scenes in films discredit the white woman in the eyes of the Africans' (my translation). G. Jahoda, *White Man*, London, Oxford University Press, 1962, p. 105, confirms this.

15. Cyprian Ekwensi, *Jagua Nana*, London, Heinemann, 1961, 1975, p. 7, p. 13.

16. Okot p'Bitek, *Song of Lawino, a Lament*, Nairobi, East African Publishing House, 1966, p. 41.

17. Arlette Chemain-Degrange, *Emancipation féminine et roman africain*, Dakar, Nouvelles Editions Africaines, 1980.

18. Francis P. Imbuga, *The Married Bachelor*, Nairobi, East African Publishing House, 1973, pp. 53-4.

19. Buchi Emecheta, *Double Yoke*, London/Ibuza, Ogwugwu Afor, 1982, pp. 154–5.
20. Buchi: Emecheta, *The Joys of Motherhood*, London, Heinemann, 1979.
21. Mariama Bâ, *Une si longue lettre*, Dakar, Nouvelles Editions Africaines, 1979,
22. The interview in the Dutch edition of the book was done by Jan Kees van de Werk.
23. P. Ngandu Nkashama, 'Le théâtre: vers une dramaturgie fonctionnelle', in: *La littérature zaïroise*, numéro spécial de *Notre Librairie*, janvier-mars 1982, pp. 67–8.
24. ibid., pp. 72–4.
25. Eleanor Wachtel, 'The Mother and the Whore: Image and Stereotype of African Women', *Umoja*, 1, no. 2, p. 42.
26. The selected papers presented at this conference were published in 1984. See Ulla Schild (ed.), *Jaw-Bones and Umbilical Cords*, Berlin, Reimer Verlag.
27. Jane Bryce, 'Book Fair Blazes Trail', *The New African*, May 1983, pp. 34–5.
28. Lloyd W. Brown, *Women Writers in Black Africa*, West port, Conn., Greenwood Press, 1981.
29. Femi Ojo-Ade, 'Female Writers, Male Critics', *African Literature Today*, 13, 1983, p. 176. See also his 'Still a Victim? Mariama Bâ's *Une si longue lettre*', *African Literature Today*, 12, 1982. pp. 71–87.
30. Ojo-Ade, 'Still a Victim?', p. 84.
31. Eustace Palmer, 'The Feminine Point of View: Buchi Emecheta's *Joys of Motherhood*', *African Literature Today*, 13, 1983, p. 39.
32. ibid., pp. 44, 55.
33. Chinua Achebe, *Morning Yet on Creation Day*, London, Heinemann, 1975, p. 6.
34. ibid.
35. A more extended version of this paper is to be found in Mineke Schipper (ed.), *Unheard Words. Women and Literature in Africa, the Arab World, Asia, the Caribbean and Latin America*; London, Allison & Busby, 1985, pp. 22–59.

Feminist Issues in the Fiction of Kenya's Women Writers

Jean F. O'Barr

Introduction

Scholars in the field of African literature rarely discuss feminist concerns. The number of novels about and by black Africans, in both European and vernacular languages, is vast; the number of reviews of African literature as a field of study is almost as extensive. Ploughing through the bibliographies, anthologies and reviews, consensus emerges among writers and commentators on two points. First, irrespective of the publisher's series, the particular country or time period, or the type of literature under consideration, female writers are few in number. If Ama Ata Aidoo, Buchi Emecheta, Bessie Head, Flora Nwapa, Grace Ogot and Efua Sutherland are listed and single works by Mariama Bâ and Rebeka Njau are added, one has almost exhausted the female writers who write in or have been translated into the English language and who are known and discussed by critics. No major anthologies of African literature include selections of works by female writers and the few that are organized by topic rather than by author make only fleeting references to women writers. Two new publications appear to be changing that trend. Lloyd Brown's book, *African Women Writers* (1981),[1] looks at the literary styles of Aidoo, Emecheta, Head, Nwapa and Sutherland. Eustace Palmer published an article on the feminine point of view in Emecheta's *The Joys of Motherhood* in the 1983 edition of *African Literature Today*.[2]

A second point that emerges from a review of African literature as a field is that gender is rarely a theme for analysis. The outline that Claude Wauthier gives in *The Literature and Thought of*

Modern Africa (1979) illustrates what most commentators say about Black African literature as a developing field. He begins by placing the emergence of literature in the general cultural revival of Africa after independence:

> Throughout history, the demand for national independence has gone hand in hand with cultural revival. One of the most striking examples of this trend is to be found in the national movement of eastern Europe during the last century. These grammarians, historians, and poets united in the struggle to revitalise the soul of their people: the grammarians, by forging a national language from a dialect, the historians, by substituting the history of a nation for that of a series of dynasties; and the poets, by exalting revolutionary struggle.
>
> The movement for emancipation in the former African colonies is no exception to this rule. Independence has been preceded there by a cultural activity which is all the more surprising in that illiteracy was the general rule in black Africa until the second world war.[3]

He then goes on to review the major themes addressed by over 150 African writers from both French and British backgrounds. He identifies the themes as cultural conflict, disillusionment with independence, and a continuing tradition of protest. He notes that the 'meeting of two civilisations, the European and the African, the shock it caused both to the individual and to the society, narrated in the form of a semi-biography or a village chronicle, has been the favourite subject of the African novelists before independence'.[4] The cultural conflict theme is so common that critics have developed typologies and shown how some authors have tried to create a new place for old beliefs, others have tried to demystify the magical features of everyday life and still others have idealized past beliefs.

Disillusionment with the post-independence era is now a major theme in African literature, according to Wauthier. He concludes his survey with the statement that African literature continues to be a protest literature:

> After the achievement of independence, African literature reflected with extraordinary sensitivity the tensions created by the discussion about the options open to the new states and their governments. The conflict between African tradition and a technical civilization, which culminated in the rebellion against colonial domination, could only become more intense once the decision about the path to be followed depended upon the Africans themselves. Thus, African literary production continued to turn on protest and conflict . . .[5]

A little imagination and a bit of feminist perspective can extend Wauthier's analysis to include women and to document their impact on African literature. Women writers emerged in the 1970s, since by then women had slightly greater access to education. Women took up the 'conflict and disillusionment' themes but extended them into new areas of social life, especially gender roles, bringing a female point of view to the issues of cultural conflict and economic change. This paper analyses the works of seven Kenyan women writers to see how they portray women's attitudes and behaviour towards contemporary gender role questions.

Kenyan women are experiencing social situations fraught with contradictions. Novelists show women responding to these conflicts with a mixture of initiative and passivity. The novels analysed here document the fact that structural constraints on the exercise of options by women is severe and that the individual solutions that women seek can be no more than temporary mechanisms allowing them to cope with the situations they face. They suggest that the next decade may see increasingly tense political debates as women move from a personal awareness of difficulties to a collective stance on remedies and how to reach them. While the novels deal with the same questions that preoccupy social analysts, they discuss the questions from the points of view of women, providing information on how women conceptualize issues and how they handle them when the changing social milieu militates against any consensus on alternatives.

By and large, the novels are stories about how individuals and communities react to changing conditions. Some plots are those of power struggles, others of the dilemmas of modernization, others remembrances of the past and one novel looks at life in Britain. A knowledge of the plots is not necessary to explaining what the novels say about strategies the women use to cope with their situation. A life cycle approach to gender role questions emerges from the stories and is employed in this paper to organize the discussion. Sociological research has shown that 'all women' cannot be grouped into a single category; rather, one must look at each woman's (or set of women's) place in the life cycle and the social structure. The novels divide themselves readily into the particular stages of women's lives: they deal with how female children become women; with what marriage means for women; with where women's work fits into their lives.

It is important to point out that this three-way categorization covers all the main issues discussed in the novels under review. The authors do not look at childhood nor at old age. Their interest is focused on the midpoints of life. While the novels frequently discuss the way in which people led their lives in the past, they do not look at those other points in the life cycle when doing so. Nor do any of the novels address the future in any form.

The Woman's Point of View

The authors all write from a woman's point of view, sharply underscoring the idea that the female perspective on social life and women's part in it may be different from the male perspective on the same topic. The characters all have some feminist consciousness. It is as if they had read the feminist research of the last two decades, learned that women are social actors with an agenda to pursue if observers would only observe them, then gone on to a women's studies lecture series and learned that without their perspective an understanding of social life was incomplete, and decided to tell how things looked from their vantage points.

By looking at social life from the points of view of women, these authors place women at the centre of their works and see them in their full complexity, dealing with multiple issues and playing multiple, indeed sometimes contradictory, roles. Consider, for example, Maria, one of the four female characters in *Ripples in the Pool* by Rebeka Njau.[6] Maria works as a nurse and in the story is asked in two separate instances to assist both factions in a power struggle. She is aware of her multiple relationships – as a lover to a man on one side, as an old friend to a man on the other, as a single working woman of forty-one years of age who is dependent on her hospital job. Maria puts off requests from each side to relay information, having studied the situation and realized that the politician who asked for her help is about to lose his position of power. Later in the story she is asked by her old friend to aid his side of the struggle. She refuses him, saying that he has never had the strength of character to be successful. She then follows through on her plan to move to another area, in opposition to the demands of both of the significant men in her life. While one might criticize Maria for running away rather than charging in to change the situation, there is no doubt that she is aware of the complexity of her place in the social network and shrewd enough to realize that if she allows herself to be used in men's power struggles, not only will she cease to be her own person, but will also not be able to depend on either of them to consider her needs in the future.

A second example can be drawn from *Your Heart Is My Altar* in which Miriam Were looks at village-level controversy between a chief and the educated young people through the eyes of a young woman who is not allowed to participate in the struggle.[7] The chief in this narrative is opposed to schooling for young people; he senses that exposure to new worlds will lessen their dependence on his world. The two older siblings of the narrator in the novel join with their peers in a plot to overthrow the chief. Throughout the novel, as the narrator struggles to move from childhood to maturity, she watches the public drama being played out. The fact that her brother and sister go to secret meetings, whisper to each other at odd moments during farm work, and tell falsehoods to her parents has a powerful impact on her view of herself and her place in the community. She transfers her rejection from their plot to a rejection of her value as a person. She lashes out at one point: 'Well, that is the way it is. I was either too young or I was kept away because I was a woman. What was there in this world for a youngster that happened to be a woman? Someday, there must be an answer'.[8] In her unhappiness with herself, she looks forward to finding a boyfriend but is wise enough to know that a boyfriend is not really the answer to her problem.

It is useful at this point in the discussion to observe that the fiction written by African men takes a far less sophisticated view of women's lives and sees them as secondary figures in the environment of males. In fact, Bonnie Barthold, in *Black Time: Fiction of Africa, the Caribbean and the United States* (1981), argues that women, as portrayed in men's books, are polarized as either the prime cause of disruption of the times or as the source of its redemption.[9] Her analysis extends beyond Africa to Caribbean and black American writers, but her point is still valid. Viewing women as unidimensional, as *either/or*, is characteristic of much of African literature. The twelve works analysed here, then, put women at the centre, even when the work would not be classified as a work about women, and give the female characters complex, goal-oriented lives to live.

Adolescence

Adolescence, marriage and work stand out as the life tasks in which the female characters deal with their options and struggle with reconciling the issues of cultural conflict and economic change as applied to them personally and to women generally. Becoming an adult woman is a key task for all girls and for the young women in these Kenyan novels. Often the task is posed in terms of whether or not to undergo circumcision.

The Christian religion, as it was introduced into Kenya in colonial times, condemned the practice. Charity Waciuma in *Daughter of Mumbi* explains it this way:

> . . . [T]he Church of Scotland missions decided they had to stamp out the circumcision of women. Instead of doing this in a subtle way, they went about it so badly that they actually increased the people's attachment to their old customs. Both the girls themselves and their parents were turned away from the Church if the girls had the operation performed.[10]

According to Waciuma, young females are placed in a tug-of-war position where they are refused membership of the 'Christian Church if they have committed the 'sin' of circumcision, and are also refused a position within their community if they are not circumcised. An uncircumcised female was considered to be 'unclean' and often not allowed to marry because 'it was believed that a girl who was uncircumcised would cause the death of a circumcised husband. Moreover, an uncircumcised woman would be barren'.[11] In *Daughter of Mumbi* the Christian school girls who had not 'been to the river' to be circumcised were segregated at school from those who had been circumcised. In the village it was the uncircumcised girls who 'became a laughing-stock, the butt of their jokes';[12] at school the tables were turned and it was the circumcised girls who were ridiculed and isolated and even prevented from advancing in their education at the Christian mission schools. The Christians were attempting to eradicate this 'barbaric' tradition but instead exacerbated the culture clash. Both circumcised and uncircumcised females were made to feel ashamed of their bodies and their sexuality.

Christianity as described in these novels is imposed not only as a religion or set of beliefs but as a total culture – Western European culture. The Western Judaeo-Christian ideas of sexuality do not include the practice of female circumcision, and missionaries are therefore appalled that such barbarism is practised. In Muthoni Likimani's *They Shall be Chastised*, the following tirade by an African Christian preacher exemplifies the typical Christian response to circumcision:

CIRCUMCISED! My daughter! By whom? WHEN? Salome circumcised? Hannah! Hannah come quickly! . . . Salome is circumcised![13]

Later in his book, Likimani writes about the Shimoni Mission's Girls' School and how its staff protected girls who ran away from their homes because they feared being circumcised. 'The missionaries always had great sympathy for those who wanted to protect their genitals from lacerations. After all, the fear of God was a far more palatable experience'.[14] Although Miss Green, one of the mission's teachers, had lived among the Kenyan people for more than twenty-five years, she still did not understand their culture or tribal tradition. When several of her girls were circumcised during the Christmas holidays, she reacted with both vehemence and sympathy:

> Circumcision! . . . That pagan custom! That horrible operation on my girls! Oh, not my sweet Monica I hope! Poor Esther! I am sure they were forced. They knew it was a bad, evil, devilish action. We taught them that. Whoever did this should be punished. They must.[15]

Miss Green wanted to punish the girls by refusing them Holy Communion and suspending them from school until they repented before the Church Council. Her intolerance of Kenyan customs and assertion that female circumcision is incongruent with Christianity illustrates how the Church, as seen by these authors, required not only acceptance of a foreign religion but a foreign culture as well. The authors argue through their characters that this debate causes women's power to decrease, for women are forced to fight a battle on two fronts: one against the narrow confines of tribal customs and the other against the equally narrow standards of the Christian culture.

Likimani makes a literary attempt at reconciliation on the issue. Mr Obidiah, the headmaster at the Shimoni Mission School realized that circumcision was not necessarily un-Christian and that, in fact, the ancient custom prepared the girls for life better than the Christian schools did. He explained this to Miss Green:

> . . . I give them the academic education. But education in how they should live, leave that to the old ladies of the village. You shout at them, and they are still naughty. You had them for years brainwashing them and they still give you problems. These old village ladies take them for just one week. Now look at them – clean, polite, grown-up, shy, obedient and worthy of any man.[16]

This idea that circumcision prepares a girl for life prevails in other pieces of literature as well. Were in *Your Heart Is My Altar* discusses circumcision as a means of preparing a girl for womanhood. In the novel, Granny says to her granddaughter, 'This is the trouble with you girls from Christian villages . . . You grow into womanhood right out of childhood and without a clue what life is all about'.[17]

Some Third World women are beginning to accept the idea that female circumcision is a tool that society employs to control women. Many believe the custom to be divisive for women yet are not ready to abandon its practice altogether. Perdita Huston interviewed Sudanese women for her book *Third World Women Speak Out*; these women expressed liberal ideas about women's rights and condemned circumcision in theory; yet they still said that they would have their daughters circumcised. Huston writes 'Clearly, these women did not yet dare to act according to their expressed convictions – a reflection of how entrenched the custom of circumcision, particularly, remains in their part of the world'.[18]

In the novels a positive view of circumcision as a social practice is put forward. For these authors, girls who undergo circumcision are transformed. They had been to the river and had come to know the mysteries involved in being women. A bond formed among the women circumcised together. 'You associate yourself with those in your circumcision age group. You work as a team . . . You are all one, helping one another,' according to Likimani.[19] Older women held a certain degree of power when circumcision took place, for it was they, as experts, who educated girls. Taking away this 'bond of womanhood' among young women and between generations means taking away one aspect of power as these novels see it. While none of the works argues explicitly in favour of retaining circumcision as a means of furthering women's solidarity, all of them clearly recognize that by removing it without providing a viable substitute for engendering a sense of community, women are deprived of a significant power base.

Thus, it is during adolescence that young women learn they will be pulled by two opposing traditions where reconciliation is not really possible.

Marriage and Social Identity

Marriage is the second and, according to these novels, the most important area in which Kenyan women work out their responses to the changing social and economic milieu. The issue is most often discussed in terms of whether and how women are social beings in their own right or whether they 'need a man' to be considered whole. While this debate is familiar to people involved in women's issues internationally, it is not one that is common to the literature written by African men and it is not one which the sociological and development studies of women in Africa have seen as central in policy formulation.

The difficult and challenging position of women that pervades the analytic literature comes through strongly in the novels being analysed here. Yet there is certainly no universal literary response to this challenge. Through the turmoil created by modernization, the balance of women's traditional identities has been upset. Each character in the literature is forced to search for a way to regain the emotional, social and moral equilibrium originally provided by traditional roles. Some characters respond to this challenge with despair, resigned to their inability to reconcile their traditional identities with the modern world. Others attempt to balance elements of traditional and modern life styles. A few women deny and even degrade their traditional African identities in favour of a totally westernized way of life. The question of how individuals redefine and reaffirm their psychological, emotional and social identity is central to the Kenyan literature being analysed here. Without exception the women in the novels take advantage of the educational, economic, and attitudinal opportunities offered by modernization. The characters neither reject modernization nor unquestioningly appropriate the past in order to redefine their identities. Instead, they accept the difficulties of a dual identity which combines elements of old and new. The difficulty of balancing this new identity and the dangers of the duality become apparent when one sees how troubled these women say they are. It seems that they are never sure how much tradition to accept in their lives: accepting too much leads to domination they cannot control; yet if they reject too much, they feel that they discard the good with the antiquated past.

All twelve novels under review deal with marriage and women's social identity as central themes. The works of Grace Ogot deal most explicitly with the dilemma of women in marriage. The main character of Ogot's short story 'The Wayward Father' in *Island of Tears* serves as a good example of dual identity. Anastasia is a modern African woman who defines herself – at least partly – in terms of her ability to earn a high wage and her western attitudes toward issues. Yet, to a large degree, Anastasia's fulfillment and sense of meaning in her life are derived from her love for her husband: 'He, if nothing else, was the fulfillment in her life. . . . To a woman this formed the foundation of joy, dearer than any material gains'.[20] Though Anastasia and her husband live a wealthy life in the city, the loss of the valuable traditional support network of the extended family that Anatasia had known as a child is a severe sacrifice for her to make. She daydreams about her losses and longs to:

> be back home where she could talk to someone about her dreams and about the gradual casualness that was creeping into her marriage. A sister-in-law back home would understand such matters and give genuine advice. The in-laws, concerned about the family name, would arrange to talk to the difficult husband, and try all ways to reconcile the family.[21]

During the most difficult period of her marriage, the time when she needs the traditional support most, she laments the loss of the ability to draw on the value of tradition as a whole:

> But how could one adhere to customs in a city, with one's roots plucked out of the family unit and left bare in the scorching sun? Everything was doomed to wither away and gradually die.[22]

Though Anastasia marries her husband Mika because she loves him dearly, she is betrayed eventually. Mika degrades the family and Anastasia's love by getting a girl half his age pregnant, then marrying her behind his wife's back. In her anger, Anastasia reveals her clear understanding of the injustices of the traditional ideas of marriage and male prerogative:

> Man was cursed by God my child; even the most loved and most respectable husband will have no shame in dragging the family name in the sordid mud. It is the lot of all women however dignified and you will learn that soon enough when you are married.[23]

Yet, Anastasia submits to her husband's power even though she recognizes it is unfair. She reasons herself into believing that she should not direct her anger at her husband, the head of the household, but at the girl who is carrying his child. In her emotional turmoil and indecision, Anastasia reaffirms her purpose in life by recommitting herself to her children. Regardless of how much Mika has destroyed her love for him, Anastasia believes that 'whichever way things go, I know for sure that my children need a home and a mother'.[24] The reader suspects that the couple's tearful reunion is motivated solely, at least on Anastasia's part, by this desire to preserve the support system of the family for the children at whatever cost to herself. Anastasia, the fictional character, does not entertain any alternatives which would have her acting on her own. She knows that she is dependent on a man and finds a way of thinking about it that rationalizes it for her. Seeing the situation of marriage and the issue of social identity in Anastasia's dilemma contributes to an understanding of how contemporary Kenyan women respond to the contradictory situations in which they find themselves.

Work

The third issue demonstrating how women define options and deal with them discussed in these twelve novels concerns work and its place in their lives. Having passed through adolescence and entered marriage, women in modern Kenya experience a work life that is on the one hand totally different from what their mothers knew and on the other hand completely without opportunities for them. Muthoni Likimani and Rebeka Njau provide excellent examples of the catch-22 of employment for Kenyan women. In her poem, *What Does A Man Want*, Likimani speaks through several women characters who express their seemingly futile efforts at being both a worker and a wife. These prolific monologues express the lack of self-worth and personal gain associated with women's struggle for a 'respected' position in the work force. The degradation and hopelessness of female employment comes through in each monologue as it discusses how work revolves around men and how women spend their lives catering to someone else's needs and whims. Invariably the women lose out and are left emotionally drained and confused. In one section an older woman laments:

I married him young
My beauty he could not escape
I married him poor
What we've, I contributed
It is my sweat
My brain too.

Now as weathered as I am
Teeth dropping down
Telling me to go
To go where?[25]

'Their' wealth becomes 'his' once she no longer appeals to him.

Another section in Likimani's book details the depressing results of a successful career woman's achievements. At a mature age she succumbs to social pressures and sets out to 'capture' a man. She suddenly feels unfulfilled as a woman without a husband or child. When she was younger she was full of confidence, stating:

> Those who wanted me
> I refused with pride
> I was earning money.
>
> Property I had
> And freedom to do
> What pleased me best.
>
> I thought they were enough . . .[26]

Like other women in her society, however, she becomes disillusioned with career success and regrets the undesirable label it has placed on her:

> Work is too much
> All by myself
> Responsible work completely alone
> I dare not be seen
> I am respected.
>
> Where the young go
> I am not welcomed.
> Where the old go
> They are all in pairs.
>
> And they do not understand.
> Men are men
> Married or not
> They remain yet men.[27]

Her endeavours have stripped her of her 'femininity'. Her ambitions and her pride must be relinquished for a husband – a man who will help her to eliminate the uniqueness she represents in her traditional society. When she finds a man who wants her he is young enough to be her son. He is the only one innocent and vulnerable enough to find her and her accomplishments appealing. She lavishes her wealth on him to keep him satisfied.

My young man drove
My car now at his disposal.

The gasoline came
From my account;
The home was mine
And so was its support;

A comfortable home
Where food was plenty;
Drinks ready
Ever in the fridge;

For my man to relax
Buying all to win his love.[28]

Regardless of her own intellectual and occupational expertise she feels she must succumb to the male-oriented standards of society. After their marriage the young man takes her gifts but offers her no love or affection in return. Her support and her business achievements seem futile at the end. In her final statement she says:

Loneliness and poverty
Were all I had
Now that he had
Sucked me dry
. . .
You selected me
You thought me worthy.
When you make me poor,
Nothing more to be consumed
It's time to remember
I am old enough
To be your mother.[29]

The four women in Rebeka Njau's *Ripples in the Pool* provide a study in contrasts for a look at women and work. Selina is the loose woman of the city who has had every man and every luxury the capital provides. In her thirties, she decides to seek security in the form of marriage to a man she can manage, and moves to the village with him. There she keeps herself aloof from local affairs, expending all her energy making demands on her husband. Miscarriages and barrenness are her lot. Madness overtakes her and she is eventually killed. Gaciru is the young sister of Selina's husband who, having failed her exams, comes to help her brother serve Selina. She works quietly, the model of an accommodating person. She can perform traditional work, yet hopes to set herself up in commerce with Selina's capital. Selina makes Gaciru the object of her love, forcing her into a sexual relationship. Gaciru dies by Selina's hand in the end. The mother, Selina's mother-in-law, warns her son against Selina's history of madness, aids her son in his successful store for a while, then leaves the novel when she believes her support is undercut by her son's refusal to 'handle' his wife according to traditional mores (i.e., to beat her). Maria, the nurse and friend mentioned above, is bound to her work and eliminates community ties for the sake of work. None of the four women work out any kind of integration between being women and being workers in the modern economy. The most successful in modern terms goes mad, the one who accommodates to the old and tries for the new is killed, the traditional mother avoids the new when the old cannot be brought in, and the modern employed woman has no personal life. The novelist's clear message is that as far as women and work are concerned, Kenyan women face a no-win situation. This is a sobering message in view of the enormous amount of sociological and policy literature that encourages women to enter employment as a means of resolving the problems of change.

Conclusion

This analysis began by asking what women see as the issues central to their lives and how they deal with them. The literary data show that Kenyan women define certain life cycle tasks – entering adulthood, getting married, finding work – as the places where the contradictory demands of old and new clash most painfully. Individual women protest against the injustices, then acquiesce, reconciling contradictions more often through avoidance than positive action. Collectively, Kenyan women, as portrayed in the novels, do not act. While sociological tracts tell us that courtship and marriage practices are changing, they are rarely as forthright as these fictional characters who tell us how psychologically devastating the experience is. While political scientists and economists argue for increasing work opportunities for women as a means of building an involved citizenry, they fail to understand the double bind of Kenyan women in a situation where the traditional culture combines with a patriarchal system to prohibit work from being a source of power. The novels are quite clear on this. While politicians and legal reformers argue for policy changes, they have little contact with the mass of women. The novels tell us that the mass of women are not even aware of these issues.

The conclusion one draws from this fiction is of a social situation that is very confused about gender roles, a situation in which people are aware of social contradictions and individually invent ways to cope with stress. The novels give no evidence of an emerging consensus on how to deal with the issues. There is an almost romantic regard for the predictability of life in the past, for the social arrangements which seemed fixed, and for the support available for women. The female characters demonstrate power-lessness vis-à-vis the choices they face at each stage: they see themselves performing traditional roles (that is, having respon-sibility for children) without traditional resources (that is, having relatives to assist and farms where they can raise produce for sale), while at the same time they are undertaking modern activities (that is, acting as wives to modern men) while being denied access to modern support systems (that is, husbands who accept the responsibilities of having wives, and employment that allows some measure of autonomy). The distrust of the new and larger social system which is encompassing them is pervasive. The distrust is based in part on lack of knowledge about how to work the new system and in part on the awareness that the system itself is based on contradictory expectations of women, expectations which when grafted on to traditional gender role arrangements produce an even more debilitating situation. These are relation-ships which the social science literature often mentions, but does not analyse as fully as these works of fiction do.

Finally, the novels suggest the beginning of a new stage in writing by and about women. If Wauthier found the literary activities of the 1950s and 1960s to signify a 'movement for emancipation' a similar phenomenon is found here. The disillu-sionment women feel about present gender role relationships is being actively expressed, extending a literary tradition and per-haps signalling the beginning of a feminist literary movement. For in articulating the inequities they experience in fictional form, Kenyan women writers are raising consciousness as well.

NOTES

1. Lloyd Brown, *Women Writers in Black Africa*, Westport, Conn., Greenwood Press, 1981.
2. Eustace Palmer, 'The Feminine Point of View, Buchi Emecheta's *The Joys of Motherhood*', *African Literature Today*, 13, 1983, pp. 38–55.
3. Claude Wauthier, *The Literature and Thought of Modern Africa*, 2nd edn, London, Heinemann, 1979, p. 17.
4. ibid., p. 304.
5. ibid., p. 352.
6. Rebeka Njau, *Ripples in the Pool*, London, Heinemann, 1975.
7. Miriam Were, *Your Heart Is My Altar*, Nairobi, East African Publishing House, 1980.
8. ibid., p. 7.
9. Bonnie Barthold, *Black Time: Fiction of Africa, the Caribbean and the United States*, New Haven, Yale University Press, 1981.
10. Charity Waciuma, *Daughter of Mumbi*, Nairobi, East African Publishing House, 1969.
11. ibid., p. 95.
12. ibid., p. 61.
13. Muthoni Likimani, *They Shall Be Chastised*, Nairobi, East African Publishing House, 1974.
14. ibid., p. 179.
15. ibid., p. 198.
16. ibid., p. 200.
17. Were, *Your Heart Is My Altar*, p. 48.
18. Perdita Huston, *Third World Women Speak out*, New York, Praeger, 1979, p. 101.
19. Likimani, *They Shall Be Chastised*, p. 109.
20. Grace Ogot, *The Island of Tears*, Nairobi, Uzima, 1980, p. 8.
21. ibid., p. 11.
22. ibid., p. 19.
23. ibid., p. 15.
24. ibid., p. 19.
25. Muthoni Likimani, *What Does a Man Want?*, Nairobi, Kenya Literature Bureau, 1974, p. 184.
26. ibid., p. 172.
27. ibid., p. 173.
28. ibid., p. 180.
29. ibid., p. 182.

The Didactic Essence of Efua Sutherland's Plays

Adetokunbo Pearce

The reputation of Efua Sutherland rests perhaps most firmly on her contribution to African theatre. Since the 1950s, she has been involved with the theatre as playwright, theatre director and founder of Ghana's foremost, and most notable experimental theatre group. Her emphasis on artistic dramatic form has been rightly noted. At times this emphasis seems so accomplished that the critic is misled into assuming that Sutherland's plays sacrifice thematic profundity for stylistic innovation.[1] Her theatrical embellishment and inventiveness which comprise an overt use of stage props, the use of the Akan language and an emphasis on audience participation do not exclude authentic meanings for the reader or the audience. Sutherland's thematic concerns in her most popular plays, *Edufa, Foriwa, and The Marriage of Anansewa*[2] range from an indictment of unscrupulous materialism to ideas on rural development, the uses of tradition, and an enquiry into the essence of true love. In all these plays, which are directed primarily towards Ghanaians, Sutherland's aims have been consistently didactic; teaching readers and audiences about the moralities of life, and how best to cope with their environment. She uses tradition and popular culture as the foundations of her plays, and through the dramatic process attempts to redefine and to refine such traditions and cultures. Her plays reflect a conviction that through the play, the writer can actually monitor as well as influence a nation's cultural direction and taste. Her conception of the theatre is very much in the spirit of some of the founding fathers of contemporary English drama who contend that:

> There is no surer evidence as to the character and fibre of a people than is afforded by the nature and quality of their popular amusements, and especially of their drama . . .[3]

and that:

> No other art so nearly touches and shapes conduct and practice. No other art can so swiftly move our thoughts and feelings, or stir our passions, or inspire and direct our actions [as drama does].[4]

Efua Sutherland's plays do not chart private ontological anxieties, but rather deal with particular social and ethical issues which involve the community. Within the structure of communal drama, the role of women is often portrayed as central. In *Edufa* it is Abena, Edufa's sister, who sets the play's tone with her impassioned song of wandering and dying. Abena's song is reinforced by the funeral chant of the female chorus. Together, these songs at the beginning of the play establish the predominant mood of painful sacrifice. The portrayal of the central issue, that of insensitive materialist pursuit, is achieved in a dialectical confrontation of extreme egotism, and near-saintly selflessness in the persons of Edufa and Ampoma respectively. The plan of the main events is revealed quite early in the play by Seguwa's objection to Edufa's treatment of his wife Ampoma:

> None I know of flesh and blood.
> Has right to stake another's life
> For his own . . . Edufa does Ampoma
> wrong. He does her wrong. (p. 11)

The event referred to here, and later given to us in flashback, relates to Edufa's megalomanic desire for perpetual life. He visits a diviner who tells him of his impending death. The diviner, however, adds that this can be averted if Edufa is able to find another to die for him. Anxious to live forever, Edufa goes in search of such a sacrificial lamb. He announces to members of his household that those who love him enough to die for him should so pledge their love. Edufa does not tell them the real consequences of this pledge, or the reasons why the topic has come up. Rather, he presents his case in a light-hearted manner. Ampoma, his wife, says she loves him enough to die for him. Sometime later, the gods descend on her, demanding that she makes true her pledge; her death, for Edufa's life.

The contrasting visions of life enacted in the play are conveyed through a dialogue of principles. This is done first by Seguwa, Edufa's aide, who argues that no faith is worth having against all reason. For her, prudence is the better part of valour. Even Edufa recognizes the worth of her character when he says to her: 'Your service and your courage these last few days have given me strength and consolation' (p. 6). Edufa's character on the other hand leaves much to be desired. He is a self-centred man whose sole concern is for material wealth and public acclaim. In his eagerness to become 'emancipated' he adopts a policy of whole-sale rejection of traditional values, and an indiscriminate acceptance of values believed to be modern and progressive. Although Sutherland does not centralize the issues of westernization versus African traditions, Edufa's standpoint amounts to embracing what is popularly regarded as western individualism. His rejection of his father's advice to be truthful and decent with all men when he declares, 'I am not all men. I am emancipated' (p. 14), implies a rejection of the community and of communal values. This selfish attitude and the belief that he is a free agent, at liberty to do as he wishes leads him to treat his father Kankam with contempt, and Samson, his mute messenger, with ultimate lack of concern.

A similar selfishness, designed to assure individual survival, lies behind the manner in which he presents his predicament to his family. He does not tell them that he is afraid to die, and that he has seen a diviner who has said his death is imminent. He does not tell them that he needs a victim, but instead presents his case as if the idea of another person sacrificing his or her life for him is a far-fetched hypothesis. Even if, as he later suggests, his original plan was to use a person less close to him than his wife to carry his burden of death, his method of using people is egocentric and evil. Furthermore, Edufa's procedure in dealing with his predicament portrays the differences between traditional methods and modern methods. As his father tells us, such news of impending danger as Edufa has heard is averted, in the traditional milieu by animal sacrifice, and the offering of cola and white calico to the needy. This measure is only temporary, as tradition does not believe that anyone can hang on to life in spite of the gods. However, in so far as the sacrifice and offering are done collectively and the people believe that the death or life of one of their members spells the same for them, the dead individual can continue to live in spirit within the group. The communal process thereby offers the individual life in the fold of the community. It is this spiritual continuity that the individualistic process – with its policy of 'winner takes all' – is unable to achieve. Edufa also excludes himself from communal protection in another way. Although the Akan are not unafraid of death, the apparent exuberance of Ampoma and the chorus of mourners is in keeping with the Akan traditional view of the funeral as a celebration. As the attitude of these women shows, funerals are meant to be memorable and exciting events, in accordance with the belief that the dead person is not exterminated, but rather translated into a purer, and more powerful plane of existence.[5] The self-centred approach that he adopts proves secretive, manipulative and vulnerable. While the communal venture compels the individual to share glory, the individualistic one allows him to enjoy his success alone. But as Edufa's experience shows, total success is often elusive, and while the collectivist is able to share the burden of his failure, the individualist is not. When he fails, he fails alone, and alone he is left to carry the weight of his failure.

In contrast to Edufa, Ampoma his wife is portrayed as sympathetic, compassionate and possessing almost divine sensibilities. At the point of death, she is preoccupied not with her own plight, but with the fate of her mother and her children, the loved ones she is forced to leave behind. She reacts sensitively to the chorus of women, showing understanding of the passion of their song. Being close to death herself, she understands intuitively and deeply the inner probings of their funeral chant. Unlike Edufa, whose judgement of affairs is always determined by fashionable opinion, Ampoma approaches life from its essence. While Edufa believes that because Senchi is not a respectable academic he cannot be aptly regarded as a poet, Ampoma astutely observes that 'He is one already, no matter how he roams' (p. 52). Ampoma is equally intelligent and compassionate in her dealings with Edufa. Although she is unaware of the full implications of her vows when she declares that she loves him enough to die for him, she approaches her fate with utmost courage and dedication when she finds out that she has condemned herself to death. The prospect of her death disturbs her, especially as she cannot guarantee the welfare of her children, yet her love for Edufa is so strong that she would die for him:

> AMPOMA: Yet how good that I should
> not be the one to live beyond
> your days I could not live
> where you are not. I could not
> live without you, my husband (p. 8).

Commenting on Ampoma's character, the critic Lloyd Brown argues that Ampoma's sacrifice is 'both a genuine sentiment, as well as a covert means of demanding respect'.[6] The implication of this analysis, to my mind, is that when Ampoma slips the waist beads around Edufa's neck, and declares the act to be a symbolic 'union of our flesh', she has in effect imprisoned him in her own death. And when she makes him promise not to remarry, she is effectively imposing a constraint on his freedom and happiness after she is gone. Such cynicism, it seems to me, exists only in Edufa's grossly hypocritical mind. Ampoma's intentions are more sincere. Her symbolic gesture with the beads both affirms her continuing love and friendship, as well as demonstrates her willingness to remain his wife even in death. When she makes Edufa promise never to remarry and risk their children's lives in the hands of a stepmother, she is implying that she would rather leave their fate in the hands of the gods, and of the community at large.

The lessons learnt from *Edufa* are manifold. The play stresses the idea that the individual operating alone has a heavier burden to bear than when he operates within a group. It stresses that such separatist tendencies often motivated by selfishness lead to malpractices, faulty behaviour and ultimate failure. On the other hand, the individual operating within a communal framework shares in the strength of the group, while he shares his burden with the group. Linked with the idea of communal participation is the notion of selflessness as a virtue. As evidenced by the experience of Ampoma, who comes out as a more admirable and stronger character than Edufa, giving strengthens and enriches, because the one who gives also takes for himself.

The theme of commitment and giving to others is the main concern in another of Sutherland's plays, *Foriwa*. In this play the theme is expanded into the conception of group self-help. *Foriwa* tells the story of a village, Kyerefaso, and its backward-looking and complacent people. The traditional ruler of the village, the Queen Mother, is herself progressive, but her ideas are always opposed by the more conservative elements of her council. This trend continues until Labaran, a visitor from the northern part of the country, throws in his lot with the Queen Mother and Foriwa, her daughter. The playwright's motive seems twofold; to show that group effort is the only really worthwhile way of achieving progress, and to demonstrate the true meaning of progress based on the proper use of tradition. She achieves the first by using not one, but three characters to advance the dramatic movement of the play. She makes the form of her play – the use of group protagonists in the persons of the Queen Mother, Labaran, and Foriwa – complement her main thematic concern – the need for group leadership and collective participation in societal development. In order to deal with the second issue of the appropriate approach to tradition and the past, Sutherland adopts an overly realistic mode in which her protagonists as simulated people are used to deliver her sermon.

The Queen Mother, Labaran and Foriwa are made to concentrate on different aspects of social improvement. Labaran's main activity revolves around attempts to make Kyerefaso self-sufficient, with its own agricultural programme, school, and medical centre. Foriwa's role as the village belle is to reject the custom of arranged marriages, and to insist on women marrying men whom they love, not those who can afford to pay their dowry. The Queen Mother, for her part, wishes that her people would commit themselves to improving their abilities and their community. These related concerns culminate in the interpretation of tradition as a force to be used for the purpose of individual and communal advancement. These matters are in turn concretised and communicated to the people of Kyerefaso at their annual ceremony of renewal.

At the annual ceremony, the people of Kyerefaso rededicate themselves to the fortitude of their ancestors, the founding fathers and mothers of their village. But the rededication of the villagers has always been mere rhetoric. The ancestors' courage and commitment to action have not been emulated, and Kyerefaso has not advanced much beyond its early beginnings. With the help of Labaran, who has already assisted some members of the village to obtain training in modern farming techniques, and who has set up a local bookstore, and Foriwa, who has set new respectable standards for women in the community, the Queen Mother successfully infuses the ceremony with real life. She is able to transform the festival from the usual parade of mere rituals into a ceremony which inspires the villagers to action, in the spirit of their forefathers.

In *Foriwa*, Sutherland's idea of theatre is fully realized. The play's structure is successfully integrated with the dominant themes of rebirth and communal involvement. Most of the play's action takes place in the vicinity of the four-branched god-tree. The tree, a symbol of vitality and change, dominates the town square, and thus indicates the vital role it has to play in the life of the village. The tree also imposes its presence on the language of the play – 'the scattering of seeds like forest trees, and the picking of fruit from living branches'. In addition, this tree of life is presented as related to the question of agricultural self-sufficiency and food for the sustenance of life, one of Labaran's major interests. The play achieves a similar synthesis with its other themes. The idea of the necessity to merge the old with the new, and the need to incorporate African values with western ones for a rounded development, as well as the need for men and women from various tribes to work together are suggested formally through character representation. The Queen Mother, by virtue of her role as traditional ruler, belongs to the African past. Foriwa, and Labaran, on the other hand, represent the new as well as the western. In addition, Foriwa, a girl educated in western values, represents emancipated woman. Labaran, being a university graduate, depicts the educated male elite with access to modern western technology. Labaran is also used to represent the outsider from another ethnic group in the country. These characters who are not typical, but rather exemplary members of the class they represent, are used to demonstrate how the best from the old and the new, from Africa and the West can be utilized to achieve formidable progress. By using three characters of equal importance to carry her message, Sutherland uses the form of collective heroism to depict the idea of group leadership and participation of the community. The Queen Mother, Foriwa, and Labaran all start working for the good of Kyerefaso on an individual basis with little success. They begin to achieve real success when they team up with one another and with the entire village of Kyerefaso.

The coup de grace of this play is dealt by the Queen Mother who seizes the opportunity of the village festival to expose the sterility of the festival rites. The rites themselves are good but they have since become outdated and unproductive. At the time they were formulated they served the purposes of the village, and the villagers who uttered the ritualistic words 'earned the right to utter them by their deeds'. As Labaran's observation also shows, the elders who formulated the festival did what was relevant for their generation. It is the duty of every generation to use its cultural heritage for its own advancement. The Queen Mother's coup is not a rejection of tradition in itself but a condemnation of the tendency of people to parade in the 'ashes of their grandfathers' glorious deeds' (p. 49). This view suggests that though tradition is the basis of culture it is ultimately meaningless, impotent 'ashes', unless it is constantly reviewed, modified, and used to advance in actual terms the needs of contemporary people in contemporary society.

Sutherland's therapy for society's survival is stated in no

oblique terms in *Foriwa*: for a people to make progress, it must do away with sexism, tribalism and classism. It must involve all its members in a communal effort to continuously rebuild itself. The members of the group must commit themselves in a practical way to the attainment of self-sufficiency, which will in turn bring them moral dignity as well as material prosperity. Tradition is the root of a people's culture, but it becomes retrogressive if treated as an end in itself. Tradition should be viewed instead as a foundation that must be built upon by each succeeding generation. The playwright's arguments which forward her therapy are conveyed by her three protagonists, The Queen Mother, Foriwa, and Labaran, and her proposed synthesis recognized by the villagers' acceptance of the challenge that the three protagonists stand for.

The *Marriage of Anansewa* represents in some way Efua Sutherland's attempt to realize her own injunction that tradition must be used constructively and contemporaneously. She uses the ancient Ananse folk-tale format to comment on current issues for the education of a modern audience. As a character, Ananse is traditionally the eternal trickster who weaves stories around his own great mental abilities and material wealth. Ananse almost invariably over-reaches himself, thus becoming the object of laughter. Traditionally Ananse's behaviour is used as an artistic device to mirror fundamental human passions, ambitions and follies. But the more serious aspect of Ananse, the essential reason why he always feels the need to outwit all around him, is survival. Sutherland's play begins by portraying Ananse in his traditional role of a comic, but we are soon told that Ananse is not the rascal that he appears to be. His actions are motivated by a strong desire to protect Anansewa, his daughter, from harm. This thoughtful aspect of Ananse seems to be Sutherland's main interest, the comical side of the character being used to win audience empathy.

The main plot of *The Marriage of Anansewa* consists of the ingenious schemes that Kweku Ananse devises to secure the most suitable husband for his daughter from a list of four suitors. Resolution is reached through a process of elimination of the suitors until only the most appropriate remains. The dramatic impetus is carried in the main by Kweku Ananse, and his attempts to avoid the wrath of the failed suitors whom he has given no reason to doubt the success of their individual bids for his daughter's hand in marriage. When he feels that his daughter has reached marriageable age, Ananse takes a trip around the countryside showing her photograph to eligible and well-to-do chiefs, inviting them to ask formally for her hand in marriage. Ananse does not, however, tell the chiefs that he has arranged a competition around his daughter. Soon after Ananse's trip, each chief, thinking he is the only suitor, sends gifts to Ananse's household to smooth the way to his being accepted as Anansewa's husband. At this stage of the negotiations, Ananse is protected by law because, as the storyteller informs us, there is no law binding Ananse to give his daughter to any of the chiefs. Ananse's position rapidly becomes less secure, however, as the chiefs in rapid succession send their emissaries to Ananse anouncing their eagerness to complete the formalities preceding the marriage proper. The play's tempo increases with the arrival of each emissary and Ananse is thrown deeper into conflict. Just as Ananse seems trapped by the snares he has set for others and is about to lose his reputation as the legendary intractable trickster, he comes up with a brainwave. He declares his daughter dead, and studies the reaction of the various suitors to this news. The one who shows continued commitment to Anansewa in 'death' will be the one who truly loves her. Ananse the apparent confidence-trickster has turned moralizer.

Both Ananse's name and character are based on those of Ananse, the Akan Spider god who is portrayed in folklore as forever spinning and acting out a succession of plots to ensnare mankind. A careful analysis of the spider god's activities, and indeed of Ananse's in Sutherland's play, reveals, however, that Ananse's motives are not in themselves evil. As we see from Ananse's test for his daughter's suitors, success or failure in life's endeavours depends largely on the individual's character. When Ananse announces the mock death of his daughter, he does not advise any of the suitors on what he would regard as the proper etiquette he expects of them. Their consequent behaviour reveals their real characters, three of them showing their unworthiness through their fundamental lack of genuine concern for Anansewa. Ananse's trial of the suitors is not itself evil, but it helps to expose the good or evil in each of the contestants. Like Esu, the Yoruba trickster god, Ananse is not intrinsically evil, but rather serves as a touchstone for the human conscience.

Technically, the play operates along a motif of multiple action, and multiple audience. As Lloyd Brown rightly observes, this structure has the effect of 'blurring the usual distinction between stage and audience, action and detached spectator'.[7] The adoption of this technique of total theatre proves rewarding. With the structural gambit, most aspects of the playwright's ideal of theatre as a living, cultural medium are achieved. The audience is able to participate both as an audience watching a play, and an audience in a play. This point is underscored by the detachment of 'property man' and 'story-teller' from the drama. In this way, though they communicate with Ananse and the other characters in the play, they identify themselves closely with the audience watching the play. Secondly, 'property man', and 'story-teller' often appeal directly to the theatre audience for their comments on the play's action, thus involving them in the drama. Having been made part of the play in this manner, the audience is able to learn from the education of Anansewa, and to check their experiences against the social issues highlighted in the play. Sutherland's intention in all three plays under review does not appear to be an attempt to develop convincing lifelike characters. She seems instead to perceive the actor's role in its original function which, as J.L. Styan reminds us, was 'not first that of impersonation, but nearer to that of interpreter and spokesman'.[8]

Ananse in The Marriage of Anansewa is even less of a hero in the realistic mode than Ampoma is in Edufa, or The Queen Mother, Labaran, and Foriwa are in Foriwa. He is drawn instead as both a character in a fable and one in a realistic play. Within the scope of the former, Ananse is portrayed as a comedian who thoroughly enjoys his antics of weaving plots and counterplots. The naturalistic portrayal of Ananse, on the other hand, shows him as a concerned father determined to teach his daughter the ways of the world. At the start of the play, Anansewa is something of a novice, but as the play progresses, she develops into an adult who is willing to take steps towards achieving self-fulfilment. As Ananse points out, it is vital for underdogs like himself and his daughter to use their wits to survive in a difficult world, especially when they are pitted against the more privileged class represented by the wealthy chiefs.

Ananse's machination enjoys the playwright's endorsement in that his motives for apparently misleading his daughter's suitors are presented, not as being malicious, but earnest. Further developments go to prove the wisdom of his actions, as three of the suitors show themselves unworthy. When he decides to invite four suitors instead of the customary one, Ananse interprets tradition constructively, and that interpretation perhaps saves his daughter from an unhappy marriage. Similarly, when Chief-who-is-chief decides to go beyond the bounds of tradition and cater for the 'funeral' of Anansewa to whom he is yet unbetrothed he adopts a positive approach to tradition. The attitude of these two represents Sutherland's ideal of the flexible and creative use of custom.

It would be easy to miss Efua Sutherland's thematic emphasis if we allow ourselves to become mesmerized by the technical elaborateness of her plays. The remedy lies in searching for messages in the very structure of the plays, and in interpreting the role of dramatis personae who are not characters built up in the conventional sense, but are in the main representative types. In *Edufa*, for example, dramatic action is structured around Ampoma's deathbed, and while she who gives her life for love represents the ideal, Edufa, the cause of her death, stands for the opposite. In *Foriwa*, action centres on the town square and its four-branched tree of life. Here The Queen Mother, Labaran, and Foriwa are made to depict the model behaviour that would lead to rejuvenated life symbolized by the god-tree. *The Marriage of Anansewa* does not present as obvious a fusion of structure and theme as do the two earlier plays. But even there, the playwright's lessons are clear enough. Victory lies with those who use tradition humanely. And just as the 'story-telling drama' is presented technically as a communal activity, experience should ideally be communally shared.

NOTES

1. See Michael Etherton, *The Development of African Drama*, London, Hutchinson, 1982, p. 196.
2. Reference is to the following editions of Efua Sutherland's plays: *Edufa*, London, Longman, 1967; *Foriwa*, Tema, Ghana Publishing Corporation, 1967; *The Marriage of Anansewa*, London, Longman, 1975.
3. Henry Arthur Jones, *The Foundations of a National Drama*, London, Chapman & Hall, 1913, p. xv.
4. ibid., p. 2.
5. See J.H. Nketia, *Funeral Dirges of the Akan People*, New York, Negro Universities Press, 1969, pp. 5-6.
6. Lloyd W. Brown, *Women Writers in Black Africa*, Westwood, Conn., Greenwood Press, 1981, p. 68.
7. ibid., p. 80.
8. J.L. Styan, *Drama, Stage and Audience*, Cambridge, Cambridge University Press, 1975, p. 141.

Bessie Head: A Question of Power and Identity

Charles Ponnuthurai Sarvan

Bessie Head's novel *A Question of Power*[1] raises the problem of how one can write about inner chaos without the work itself becoming chaotic. (There are similar difficulties in, for example, writing about tedium without becoming tedious; about meaninglessness without losing meaning.) One is reminded of Mary Turner in Doris Lessing's *The Grass is Singing*; of Oskar in Günter Grass's *The Tin Drum* (*Die Blechtrommel*); of Malcolm Lowry's *Under the Volcano*; of Saul Bellow's *Herzog* and, closer in time and distance, of Zimbabwe's Dambudzo Marechera and his *Black Sunlight*. Both Marechera and Head write about the cruelty done to individuals and the damage they consequently suffer. They are hunted and haunted writers whose works are an attempt to understand and come to terms; a wrestle to win through, out and above. Pauline Smith wrote that human beings sometimes have to endure the unendurable: Bessie Head writes of the human 'capacity to endure the excruciating'. Appropriately, the novel is set in a village called Motabeng, 'the place of sand'. Motabeng suggests a lack of certainty and firmness. Like life and the world, all is loose, shifting and changing. Yet we search for little rocks and patches of firm ground in the sand; for permanence within the wider impermanence; for value within the ultimate valuelessness.

To understand this strongly autobiographical work, one must know something of Bessie Head's life, even though it is painful to record it. Bessie Head was born in Pietermaritzburg, South Africa in 1937. Her Scottish mother (belonging to a wealthy family) fell in love with the African groom and shortly after was committed by the family to an institution. Bessie Head was born in the asylum's hospital and was first given to an Afrikaner family to foster, but they soon rejected her because she was not sufficiently white. She was then handed over to a Coloured family but, after a while, her Coloured foster mother was considered unsuitable to care for the child and Bessie Head was moved to a mission orphanage. She studied at high school and later pursued a teacher-training course. She worked as a teacher and then as a journalist for *Drum* magazine. She married Harold Head but the marriage ended in divorce and in 1963, more for personal than political reasons, Bessie Head left South Africa on an exit permit. (An exit permit allows a citizen to leave South Africa but not to return.) From then until her death in April 1986 she lived and worked in Serowe, Botswana, a stateless person.[2] That despite these formidable circumstances, Bessie Head wrote three novels, a collection of short stories and a work on Serowe, is a testimony to rare personal courage and to a talent which would not be stifled.

The central character in *A Question of Power* is Elizabeth, and the novel covers a little more than a year in her life (around 1970) a time when she experienced a nervous breakdown and was committed to an asylum. The hallucinatory is real to Elizabeth and therefore presented as factual. The reader is placed within her world, and experiences something of Elizabeth's bewilderment and strain. Such a subject was foreshadowed in *Maru*[3] where the characters, whilst being individuals, also represent forces. That novel confronts the mystery and power of man, the extraordinariness within the apparently ordinary. People were 'horrible' to Maru because he could see into their thoughts and feelings, see their very bloodstreams and hear the beating of their hearts. The novel goes beyond psychology and dreams to the psychic and the supernatural. Not only are Maru and Moleka aspects of one person, but within the half of Maru there are further divisions such as between his compassion and idealism on the one hand, and his cruelty and cunning on the other. The interest in psychic states, Margaret's nightmares, her awareness of something within her 'more powerful than her body could endure' all prepare us for the fracture which is the subject of *A Question of Power*. 'But there was a depth of secret activity in him like that long, low line of black, boiling cloud. There was a clear blue sky in his mind that calmly awaited the storm in his heart . . . ' (*Maru*, pp. 7–8). To say that *A Question of Power* is about one 'fall' or breakdown is to oversimplify the novel. The work describes a series of defeats and successes and, in this way, more truthfully represents the pattern of human life. 'The dawn came. The soft shifts and changes of light stirred with a slow wonder over the vast expanse of the African sky.' (p. 100). But dawn and night alternate and in the experience of some, the nights are more frequent and longer.

In South Africa, the Africans 'live the living death of humiliation'.[4] Elizabeth 'had also lived the back-breaking life of all black people in South Africa. It was like living with permanent nervous tension . . .' (p. 19). The simple joys of being a human being are denied to non-whites. As a new pupil, Elizabeth is told by the European principal of the missionary school: 'Your mother was insane. If you're not careful you'll get insane . . . They had to lock her up, as she was having a child by the stable boy . . .' (p. 16). Escaping from the cruelty and madness of that country, Elizabeth comes to Botswana. The British 'protectorate' of Bechuanaland was granted internal self-government in March 1965 and in the following year became the independent state of Botswana (30 September 1966). If one includes Namibia which is presently occupied by South Africa, one could say that the country is almost surrounded by South Africa. On its north, Botswana was flanked by a white settler government until replaced by an independent Zimbabwe on 18 March 1980. Thus the Botswana of Bessie Head's novels is very much under the shadow of apartheid South Africa.

As a Coloured, a descendant of African and European parents, Elizabeth finds herself in a racial no-man's land. The majority of European 'experts' and volunteers take the inferiority of the black man for granted and 'don't see the shades and shadows of life on black people's faces.' (p. 82). Elizabeth resents this but is herself half-European, and with her South African colour conditioning, is in danger of sharing racial opinions and attitudes. 'You don't like the African hair. You don't like the African nose . . .' (p. 48):

> 'You don't really like Africans. You see his face? It's vacant and stupid . . . You have no place here. Why don't you go away . . . ' She sprang to her feet . . . and shouted: 'Oh, you bloody bastard . . . Batswana!' (p. 51)

Committed to an asylum, Elizabeth is asked to join the other inmates in keeping the place clean, but she refuses, demanding different treatment because 'I'm not an African' (p. 181). However, Elizabeth's real desire is for acceptance by Africans as an African:

> I dearly loved Robert Sobukwe and the politics he expounded in the years 1958–60 . . . Sobukwe's view was Pan African and generally

included all things African, with an edge of harshness in it that forced one to make an identification with being African and a sense of belonging to Africa . . .[5]

Despite having lived simply in a village for many years and participating in communal work, Elizabeth remains 'an out-and-out outsider' to the people of Motabeng. One of the tormenting voices within her jeers at her because she doesn't know an African language (p. 44); taunts her with not being 'genuinely African' (p. 159). ' "We don't want you here. This is my land. These are my people. We keep our things to ourselves . . ." ' (p. 38).

Past experiences make Elizabeth reluctant to repose confidence in others. She is afraid of disappointment; afraid of the sudden revelation of violence or ugliness. Yet by nature she is given to spontaneity, impulsive affection and trust. So too, the natural sensuality within her is repressed: much of her nightmare is overtly sexual. Elizabeth believes that, in extreme contrast to herself, the Africans are a potent and promiscuous people.

> The social defects of Africa are, first, the African man's loose, carefree sexuality; it hasn't the stopgaps of love and tenderness and personal romantic treasuring of women. It is just sex . . . the women have a corresponding mental and physical approach. (p. 137)

Bessie Head herself seemed to share this view:

> The clarity of Doris Lessing's political thought arouses profound respect . . . [But] I disliked the image of a woman continually in bed with men she despises. It's just a waste . . . I cannot endure the waste of trifling love affairs.[6]

Tom, the American, has another perspective: 'This is one of the most unobscene societies in the world. Men just sleep with women, and that's all there is to it.' (p. 161). But Elizabeth associates sex with sadism, dirt, child molestation, incest, homosexuality and intercourse with animals: 'everything was high, sexual hysteria' (p. 160). Elizabeth's obsession with sex and her attitude to it are conditioned by her childhood. Growing up in a 'beer house' frequented by prostitutes and drunken (often violent) men, it is not surprising that Elizabeth has a distaste for sex and that she represses the instinct within her. Her husband was promiscuous, forcing his attentions on women and sexually consorting with men. He confirmed rather than mended attitudes formed in the 'beer house' and sex became 'hell' to Elizabeth (p. 64).

In her deep distress, Elizabeth does not have the sustaining strength of religious belief. *The Bible* 'meant damn-all' and, like Makhaya in *When Rain Clouds Gather*, Elizabeth 'cared not two bits about an old man in the sky'.[7] Evil appears to be the stronger force and 'patterns of goodness were too soft, too indefinable to counter the tumultous roar of evil.' (p. 159). And so we come to the novel's title: it is a question of power. Power is associated with evil and opposed to love. The contraries are Satan and God; evil and good; power and love. But passion has power and is also therefore a force to be controlled. 'Salvation' is to be sought through a more spiritual love, and relationships that are beneficent. 'Love is two people mutually feeding each other, not one living on the soul of the other, like a ghoul.' (p. 13). But the spiritual is *not* to be sought in God but in man:

> And love was like a girl walking . . . with the wind blowing through her hair. And love was like a girl with wonder in her eyes. And love was like a girl with a flaming heart and impulsive arms . . .
> They pray, so falsely: from the heart of God let love enter the hearts of men, thus removing the things of the soul to some impossibly unseen, mystical heaven. (p. 54)

Since power is evil, politics which is concerned with power, is also rejected in favour of a political laissez-faire.

The excruciating nature of Elizabeth's experience makes this novel, the record of a 'nightmare soul-journey', a very difficult work to read. To portray individuals at a mental extremity is a very difficult task. Elizabeth's inability to sleep and the fact that when she does, it is only to be tormented by nightmares, leave her exhausted physically and mentally. In the mornings, Elizabeth often finds herself on the floor, having rolled off the bed in her nightmare struggles. Desperate for sleep, she is afraid to close her eyes because of the voices and visions which take over. Her little son makes a paper aeroplane and says, 'I'm afraid of the edge' for he believes the plane will tumble off the edge of the world. Elizabeth has half-fallen off the edge and is struggling to climb up. Her world is inhabited by beings who are more real to her than the men and women she encounters in Motabeng, beings such as the destructive Dan Molomo ('the king of sex'); the Father; a half-mad Asian and Sello. Sello himself consists of two beings, one a monk and passive; the other a figure of evil. Towards the end of the novel, Sello and Dan seem to coalesce and become one, suggesting that they are aspects of Elizabeth herself.

Elizabeth wins through by using weapons and defences of her own. The work she engages in is meaningful: her first employment is as a teacher. The children she taught were thin as the 'twisted thorn-bush' but they were eager to learn. The school was the 'only sane centre of purposeful . . . and hopeful activity in this desolation'. (p. 68). Dismissed by a malicious and petty headmaster, Elizabeth takes to market gardening. Earlier, she had been troubled by the thought that she did not have an adequately developed and active social conscience:

> At this gesture, a group of people walked quietly into the room. They were the poor of Africa . . . They said nothing, but an old woman out of the crowd turned to Elizabeth and said: 'Will you help us? We are a people who have suffered.' (p. 31)

Now Elizabeth feels that in growing vegetables, in learning and imparting better techniques, she is making a modest but valuable contribution towards the needy of this world. On the farms, she meets not only agriculturists from different parts of the world but plants alien to the country, yet thriving. The work has a 'melody' (p. 153), a harmony, and if 'a complete stranger' like the Cape Gooseberry could 'settle' down, why couldn't an exile like Elizabeth eventually find sanctuary, a home? Agriculture can be a solitary activity but Elizabeth works on co-operative, experimental projects. This means that she is working *with* others.

Though not a Christian, there is a strong spiritual, almost mystical element in Elizabeth: the influence of Hinduism and Buddhism. Love is not of god but of man and for man. God is but another word for that nobility, understanding and compassion of which man is capable. Love is the realization of grandeur potentially there within human beings (p. 35); love is the 'gentle remodelling' (p. 136) of broken personalities.

In this way, through a lifting response to nature – even to its austere beauty – through physical labour, co-operative work, through human fellowship, a belief in the goodness of man, through understanding, compassion and love for one's fellow beings, Elizabeth overcomes those forces which sought to annihilate her.

> I felt that I would go through this experience again were I re-born . . .
> My desperate terror then was that if I recorded the evil and the same story was about to happen in some other life, I would read *A Question of Power* and it would save me from such suffering . . . My novels and I never came in from the cold. They remained in the village building up

pathetic little rural industries and co-operatives in the hope that they would expand the world and open new doors. The books stayed with the people who were in the cold.[8]

But Elizabeth does come in from the cold, though not totally and finally. She resolves the question of identity: to identify herself with Africans was, after all, to identify herself with mankind. Black power is 'a power that belongs to all of mankind and in which all mankind can share.' (p. 135). She who suffered exclusion will not, in her turn, exclude anyone. Elizabeth throws away the tablets with which she had intended to commit suicide and, 'as she fell asleep, she placed one soft hand over her land. It was a gesture of belonging.' (p. 206). 'Power' has been understood; identity accepted and extended but, of course, the 'Question(s)', as ever, remain. The novel is the work of an honest, sensitive and courageous writer.

NOTES

1. Page references in the text – unless otherwise stated – are to Bessie Head, *A Question of Power*, London, Heinemann, 1974.
2. I owe much of the above information to Jean Marquard's 'Bessie Head: Exile and Community in Southern Africa', *London Magazine*, 18, nos 9 & 10, Dec 1978/Jan 1979, pp. 48–61.
3. Bessie Head, *Maru*, London, Heinemann, 1972.
4. Bessie Head, *When Rain Clouds Gather*, London, Heinemann, 1969, p. 126.
5. Bessie Head, letter to the present writer, 25 April 1980.
6. ibid.
7. Head, *When Rain Clouds Gather*, p. 131.
8. Bessie Head, letter to the present writer, 26 June 1980.

Contemporary Society and the Female Imagination: A Study of the Novels of Mariama Bâ

Mbye B. Cham

'... there is a cry everywhere, everywhere in the world, a woman's cry is being uttered. The cry may be different, but there is still a certain unity,' stated the late Senegalese novelist, Mariama Bâ, in an interview following the Noma Award in 1980 for her first novel *Une si longue lettre*.[1] The nature of this cry ('a cry from the heart') and its implications – personal, social, psychological, cultural, political and economic – constitute the principal focus of *Une si longue lettre* and *Un chant ecarlate*,[2] her second novel published posthumously in 1981. In detailing the nature and implications of this universal feminine cry on the African soil, both novels explore at the same time a dominant issue whose persistent recurrence in recent years in the works of African and Afro-American female writers, in particular, is somewhat disproportionate to the volume and quality of its treatment in the critical literature. This issue is itself a symptom of the confusion that has occurred in the spectrum of relations between women and men in society. For want of a more comprehensive and better-sounding label, we shall refer to it as one of abandonment, with all that it entails on the personal, social, psychological, cultural, political and economic levels.

Abandonment in the novels of Mariama Bâ is predominantly a female condition. It is both physical and psychological, and it transcends race, class, ethnicity and caste. Hence the universality of this cry of the woman subjected to this condition. The forces in society that set in motion the process that culminates in abandonment and the resultant impact of such a process on the abandoned female are conceived by Mariama Bâ to be enormously out of proportion to each other. The whim or accidental fancy of the male and the calculated machinations of a female elder, translated into reality either willingly or reluctantly by the male, place upon the female a burden infinitely heavier than the cause of that burden. The response to this unexpected burden takes one of two forms: reluctant surrender and a decision to bear the burden while lamenting and exposing social and other kinds of ills, or categorical refusal to shoulder the burden and a determination to opt for freedom through various means. In either case, however, the female will and determination to live and to retain the integrity of her moral principles usually predominate. Herein lies the faith and confidence of Mariama Bâ in a better future for women, in particular, and humankind, in general.

Posed in this manner, the issue of abandonment in the novels of Mariama Bâ begins to take on the characteristics of a power struggle in which both sides, male as well as female, invoke canons of indigenous traditions as well as adopted non-indigenous values (conceived of as 'universal') to justify or contest attitudes, beliefs and actions. More specifically, the novelist concentrates on the question of the misuse and distortion of power and privilege in a socio-cultural milieu in which one segment of the population – male, acting independently or under pressure from outside forces such as parents motivated by profit or revenue – readily acknowledges but selfishly and deceptively perverts privileges bestowed upon it by tradition to the detriment and disadvantage of the female segment. The two possible responses to this selective adherence to tradition – selective because it acknowledges privileges yet shirks responsibilities and obligations that come with such privileges – defines the nature, the intensity, the parameters and the outcome of this power struggle. In the light of this, one can thus dismiss right away the stereotype of the docile traditional African woman who mutely and passively surrenders to the whims and dictates of the African man. The very idea of a response suggests some measure of consciousness which, in the case of Mariama Bâ's heroines, is translated into various kinds of concrete actions designed, in most cases, to counteract the potentially devastating condition of physical and psychological abandonment.

Power struggle, then, is to be seen not so much in terms of victory/defeat, since it is the kind of struggle that yields a no-win situation, but is to be looked at from the perspective of the impact of the experience on the individual and the latter's ability to examine, articulate and utilize the transformative capabilities of such an experience of struggle. The heroines in *Une si longue lettre* – Rama, Aissatou and Jacqueline – are a living testimony to the positive transformative capabilities of a negative experience born of the problem of abandonment. Each one emerges from basically the same experiences stronger and better placed to understand more clearly, cope with, analyse and articulate the problems, challenges and aspirations not only of women, but also of society in general. Such is the nature of the dialectical mind of Mariama Bâ. On the other hand, the white French heroine of *Un chant ecarlate*, Mireille de La Valée, exemplifies the tragedy and destruction attendant on the problem of abandonment. Her response is qualitatively different from that of the heroines of *Une si longue lettre* even though the experience that elicits the response is the same. Here, Mariama Bâ introduces the pivotal role of culture in the formulation and execution of responses to a given problematic.

Une si longue lettre derives much of its form and substance from the Islamic precept of 'Mirasse', just as the cultural concept embodied in the Wolof proverb, 'Kou wathie sa toundeu, toundeu boo feke mou tasse' (When one abandons one's own hillock, any hillock that one climbs thereafter will crumble), influences much of the form and substance of *Un chant ecarlate*. 'Mirasse' is, in essence, an Islamic religious as well as juridical principle that defines and stipulates in precise mathematical terms the nature of inheritance in the Islamic family, be it monogamous or polygamous. This notion of inheritance, laid out in the chapter on women in the Holy Qu'ran, implies disclosure of all known and unknown or secret material possessions of a deceased for division among survivors. Mariama Bâ invokes this aspect of 'Mirasse' in the case of the estate of Modou Fall, the deceased husband of Rama and Binetou in *Une si longue lettre* to outline the manner in which his estate is divided. Of much more interest and importance to our examination, however, is the skill with which Mariama Bâ extends and adapts the notion of disclosure embodied in the concept of 'Mirasse' to encompass material possessions as well as the non-material attributes and history of the individual. In extending the conceptual boundaries of 'Mirasse', the novelist is able to provide Rama with the structural and, indeed, cultural framework within which to undertake a comprehensive exposition ('dépouillement') of intimate secrets of married life with Modou Fall, particularly the latter's weakness as a human being and the effect of this on their relationship. Being such a devout Muslim, Rama sees this stocktaking as a religious duty mandated by the Qur'an: ' "Mirasse", decreed by the Qur'an, requires that a deceased individual be stripped of all his or her most intimate secrets. Thus is revealed that which was carefully concealed.' (*USLL*, p. 19).[3] 'Mirasse', therefore, becomes the principle that legitimises and regulates Rama's act of systematic personal revelation which simultaneously constitutes a systematic analysis of some of the most pressing socio-economic and cultural issues challenging women and society.

On the other hand, the narrative flow and substance of *Un chant ecarlate* is, to some extent, influenced by the Wolof proverb quoted right at the end of the novel by Ousmane's father, Djibril Gueye. This proverb which posits the equation 'abandonment of one's culture equals destruction' (kou wathie sa toudeu, toundeu boo feke mou tasse': 'wathie' – abandon; 'tasse' – crumble) succinctly captures the essence of the tragedy of Ousmane Gueye and his French wife, Mireille, whose slide toward mutual destruction is narrated in the novel. Mireille goes against, or is driven by, her domineering chauvinistic father to marry outside her race and class, and Ousmane initially sees the white woman, that paragon of beauty and perfection, as the best way to gain social recognition and status, especially in the eyes of Oulaymatou Ngom, the Senegalese girl with whom he had been madly in love since childhood but who had rejected him then. Both Mireille and Ousmane abandon or irreverently flout the canons of their respective heritage only to find out that there are none sturdy enough to serve as replacement.

It is necessary at this point to reiterate and refine the notion of abandonment as an issue in the socio-cultural settings of *Une si longue lettre* and *Un chant ecarlate*. Abandonment is not the result of a single act even though it may be a unilateral act, nor is it to be confused with divorce or repudiation even though it may share with the latter certain causal factors. Abandonment is a social disease. It is the cumulative result of a process that could be referred to as the gradual opening and enlargement of the emotional/sexual circle that originally binds two partners (a husband and a wife) to introduce and accommodate a third partner (a second wife) in a manner so devious and deceptive that a new process is set in motion. This new process itself culminates in a state of mind and body that forces the first female partner to re-evaluate the whole relationship by either reluctantly accepting or categorically rejecting the enlarged circle. It is in these twin processes that Mariama Bâ imaginatively captures the essential thoughts, feelings and actions of women and men and the impact and meaning of these for Senegalese social development.

The primary reality of the women in *Une si longue lettre* and *Un chant ecarlate* is a reality of abandonment and, more importantly, of the need and resolve to transcend and overcome it. It is most of all a reality of struggle to eliminate the root causes of this ill. Rama, Aissatou and Jacqueline in *Une si longue lettre* and Mireille in *Un chant ecarlate* are women who have had to face and contend with this reality and challenge. Rama is abandoned by Modou Fall, her husband of twenty-five years, in favour of a younger wife, Binetou; Aissatou is asked by her husband Mawdo to accept a younger co-wife, but she refuses; Jacqueline, an African from the Ivory Coast who disregards her parents' opinion about marrying a non-Ivorian, is abandoned by her playboy Senegalese husband, Samba Diack, who makes no secret of his preference for 'les fines sénégalaises' over what he and his fellow Senegalese chauvinists refer to as 'gnacs'; Mireille, the white French woman who also goes against the word of her parents and commits a sacrilege against both race and class by marrying a Senegalese blackman, is abandoned by Ousmane Gueye whose irresistible but misguided urge to prove his 'négritude' drives him blindly and tragically toward his Senegalese childhood sweetheart, Oulaymatou Ngom.

Rama reluctantly accepts and suffers this reality until the death of her husband, at which point she begins to chart a new direction and fashion a new and more resolute image of herself. Aissatou categorically rejects this reality and creates a totally different one for herself the moment she is confronted with the prospect of abandonment. In fact, in addition to being a close friend and confidante, she also becomes the stable reference point against which Rama measures her own temporary condition of instability. Jacqueline succumbs temporarily to a severe case of depression only to emerge from it a new woman. Mireille, for her part, attempts the ultimate solution when she goes completely mad, kills her baby and stabs Ousmane in an attempt to kill him after verifying the existence of a secret Senegalese co-wife.

The cumulative experience of these women, then, underscores the dialectic of oppression and struggle/regeneration that is one of the distinguishing features of the work of Mariama Bâ, and this dialectic itself undergirds the basic structure of both novels. Within the framework of this dialectic emerges the social, political and cultural vision of Mariama Bâ. It is this framework that also enables us vividly to come to terms with what, according to the novelist, constitutes one of the formidable challenges to development, namely, the warped and exploitative relationship between man and woman in contemporary Senegalese society.

One common thread binds the experiences of Rama, Aissatou and Mireille in their situation as abandoned wives. This common thread is the antagonistic role of their in-laws in the process of abandonment, and specifically, the role of the mother-in-law in turning the heads of their married sons for personal material gain and social profit. These modern-day feminine reincarnations of the spirit of Iago are exemplified in the characters of Tante Nabou, the mother-in-law of Aissatou in *Une si longue lettre* and Yaye Khady, the mother-in-law of Mireille in *Un chant ecarlate*. The machinations of these two in-laws are juxtaposed with the thoughts and actions of Modou Fall acting under the influence of lust and vanity, and those of Ousmane, a victim of cultural narcissism. Together, they present a comprehensive picture of the dynamics and nuances of abandonment. In this way, Mariama Bâ is able to bring into sharp focus the part played by both male and female segments of society in this process.

Tante Nabou and Yaye Khady are prisoners of canons of tradition considered by Mariama Bâ to be anachronistic and inimical to socio-economic transformation. She is by no means alone in this view, for a cursory search in Senegalese fiction will reveal a Yaye Bineta (La Badiène) in Sembène Ousmane's *Xala*, and Yama Diop in Aminata Sow-Fall's *Le Revenant*. Tante Nabou's sense of caste is used as a veil to perpetuate her hold on Mawdo, her 'seul homme', and to take her revenge on Aissatou, a no-good blacksmith, while Yaye Khady sees Mireille as a usurper and a loss.

Tante Nabou's *démarche* is cool and subtle, quite in consonance with the canons of comportment of her noble origin. Her relationship with Aissatou is cold and antagonistic. She looks down a long 'geer' (noble) nose on this upstart 'tegg' (blacksmith) from whom it is her honourable mission to wrest her son whose caste sin she cannot bear to live with. Her strategy is a study in calculated trickery, evident in the manner in which she manipulates her brother, niece and son to wipe out what she considers a stain on the honour of the family.

Mariama Bâ uses Rama's experience to denounce the practice of child marriage which normally receives the blessings of women, especially mothers, who see marriage uniquely as a means of social mobility and material enrichment. Rama sees Binetou, her rival of the same age as her own daughter Daba, as 'a lamb sacrificed, like many others, on the altar of materialism' (*USLL*, p. 60). Victims of male lust and vanity, victims of female greed and rivalry, these little lambs of the like of Binetou and Ngone in Sembène Ousmane's *Xala* become pawns in these useless and destructive adult games that invariably end by negatively affecting the educational and experiential development of the children. In the process, the institution of marriage is also distorted and the moral integrity and judgement of individuals who, for the most part, occupy high places of administrative, political, economic, religious and moral responsibility in the life of their communities, is compromised.

For Modou, Binetou is seen less as a partner with whom to build a life committed to a social, political, philosophical or moral ideal than a mechanism for 'rejuvenating' himself and being 'in' in the eyes of his contemporaries. For Binetou's mother, Dame Belle-Mère, Binetou is seen less as a daughter to be steered and encouraged to fulfil herself in all areas of life than a bait to land a big catch, Modou, who will deliver her and her kin from poverty. Dame Belle-Mère finds in Modou a milch cow that will instantly catapult her to the social category of 'women with heavy bracelets whose praises are sung by griots' (*USLL*, p. 74).

Her accession to and membership of this elite sorority last only as long as Modou, the foundation and the source, continues to function. When Modou passes away, the foundation crumbles and the source dries up, triggering the 'excommunication' of Dame Belle-Mère from this sorority back to her humble origins. Binetou comes out a loser as well since she becomes a child widow with little marketable educational or professional skills, a fact which condemns her to the ever-swelling corps of women at the mercy of the whims and lust of unscrupulous men, both married and unmarried. Thus, the greed and vanity of Dame Belle-Mère do not only contribute to the destruction of Rama's marriage, they also boomerang on her. Rama's daughter, Daba, shows no mercy for Dame Belle-Mère and insists on her vacating the villa which Modou Fall had ostensibly given them but which actually turns out to be legally in the name of both Modou and Rama who signed for the bank loan that bought the house. Daba replies to Dame Belle-Mère's pleas with this sober reminder:

> Remember that I was your daughter's best friend. You turned her into a rival of my mother. Remember. For five years, you deprived a mother and her twelve children of their source of support. Remember. My mother suffered a lot. How can one woman destroy the happiness of another woman? You deserve no mercy. Move out. As for Binetou, she is a victim, your victim. I pity her. (*USLL*, p. 123)

Is Mariama Bâ hereby absolving Modou of any responsibility in this drama of abandonment? The answer is, obviously, no. The part played by Modou in bringing about the situation criticized by Daba is amply detailed in the novel. It seems the novelist is more interested in probing the disturbing phenomenon of victims victimizing victims. Hence Daba's rage at the opportunistic and usurper mentality of the likes of Dame Belle-Mère who use their female offspring primarily for material gain.

Yaye Khady, Ousmane Gueye's mother in *Un chant ecarlate*, belongs to this same category of in-laws who meddle in the affairs of their sons and daughters with destructive results. The cool antagonism that characterizes the relationship between Tante Nabou and Aissatou in *Une si longue lettre* is also evident in the relationship between Yaye Khady and her white daughter-in-law, Mireille. The antagonism manifested by both mothers-in-law is based on tenets of cultural ideology: caste in the case of Tante Nabou, caste and race (i.e. culture, in general) on the part of Yaye Khady. While Tante Nabou's primary motivation is to restore the caste and class dignity of the family ('le sang est retourné à sa source'), Yaye Khady is driven mainly by a profit motive, so that the caste, racial or cultural rationalization of her antagonistic attitude becomes merely a mask, as is the case with Ousmane when, after hooking up with Oulaymatou, he states: 'I did well to renew the contact! It's my return to the sources' (*UCE*, p. 158), an obvious swipe at vulgar negritude.

The antagonistic attitude of Yaye Khady, cool and subtle at first, gradually becomes more intense and vicious as the material gains she anticipates from Ousmane's marriage elude her more and more. For Yaye Khady, Mireille is a cultural outcast, an intruder and a usurper of what she considers her cultural privileges and material payoffs. Because of Mireille, she will not be 'paid back' (double or triple, as is customary) all the money and gifts she has invested in other peoples' marriage, birth or death ceremonies. Mireille deprives her of one of the supreme moments of life for her: 'one of the high points in the life of a woman is the choice of a daughter-in-law' (*UCE*, p. 112) and all that this entails both materially and from the point of view of social prestige. For these reasons, she decides to fight the marriage, ostensibly to save Ousmane from cultural insanity, but really to promote her own self-interest. No sooner do Ousmane and Mireille set foot in Dakar after their secret wedding in Paris than Yaye Khady embarks upon her crusade ('I have work . . . ' *UCE*, p. 103) to wreck the marriage and 'dislodge' Mireille ('By whatever means necessary I will one day dislodge you' *UCE*, p. 150).

In spite of everything undertaken by Yaye Khady, Mireille still has a tenuous hold on Ousmane, but with the introduction of Oulaymatou, a new and more decisive dimension is added to Yaye Khady's scheme. Blinded by Ousmane's success and driven by the urge to partake of this success, Oulaymatou embarks upon a quest to conquer the same man whom she had ridiculed and humiliated earlier on in life. Her mother, Mère Fatim Ngom, gives her blessing and lends a big hand to such a project.

The portrayal of Yaye Khady, Mère Fatim and Tante Nabou should not, however, be interpreted to mean that Mariama Bâ hates mothers-in-law, or is anti-tradition, as may be the case with other writers from other societies. What she does is to indict the misuse of the privileges of tradition and of the institution of the mother-in-law, in particular, for personal profit at the expense of the well-being of the children-in-law. That she uses young female voices to directly attack the likes of these meddling in-laws is not surprising, given the faith and confidence she has in the effort of women to correct the situation. Just as she uses Daba to unequivocally spell out to Dame Belle-Mère the consequences of her selfish actions, so does she resort to another young woman, Soukeyna, Ousmane's younger sister, to confront Yaye Khady directly for not helping Mireille cope with her 'double apprenticeship: that of conjugal life, and that of being the wife of a black man in Africa' (*UCE*, p. 151). Mireille's efforts to integrate into the family and conform, to the best of her ability, to the Senegalese model of a good daughter-in-law fall victim to Yaye Khady's mockery, obsession with privilege and rigid preconceived notions about white women, in general.

When elders lose their sense of responsibility and self-restraint and lapse into uncontrolled excesses, then children are thrust forward to assume the role of moral arbiters. In the process, established cultural codes regulating communication and conduct between elders and youngsters are shattered. Thus, respect for elders, one of the central pillars of any society, runs the risk of becoming a casualty of the process of abandonment. This is evident in the reaction of Rama to her daughter's boldness toward Dame Belle-Mère, in Yaye Khady's shock at Soukeyna's 'hardiesse' and, in another context, the dismay of El-Hadj Abdou Kader Beye when confronted by his daughter Rama on the subject of his polygamous beliefs and practices in *Xala*.

Mariama Bâ provides a positive model of the mother-in-law in the person of Rama in *Une si longue lettre*. Rama feels no urge to intervene in the affairs of her pregnant school-age daughter, Aissatou. Her main concern is with the unfairness of a system that will penalize a school-age girl for getting pregnant while leaving the other party, the male party, untouched. Faced with this situation, Rama's motherly instinct of support and protection for a child in trouble gets the better of her, and this is made easier by Ibrahima Sall's sense of respect and devotion to Aissatou and her family. She readily forgives her daughter's mistake and resolves to help them on the difficult road ahead. Most of all, she refuses to imprison her daughter in her own value system, realizing the limits of parental control over offspring in today's society: 'I accepted my subordinate role. The ripe fruit must fall from the tree' (*USLL*, p. 125).

The phenomenon of women deliberately and maliciously sabotaging the happiness of other women in a male-dominated society is one that has come to be a major focal point in the work of Mariama Bâ and that of her compatriot, Aminata Sow-Fall. Daba's question to Dame Belle-Mère in *Une si longue lettre*, 'How can one woman destroy the happiness of another woman?' is constantly implied in *Un chant ecarlate* where friends and colleagues of Ousmane, such as Rosalie, ponder over the implications of this phenomenon. What is the state of a society, the novelist seems to be asking, in which the likes of Oulaymatou Ngom fail, or do not even want, to question male vanity and excess, especially in the area of mate-sharing? Rosalie is even more disgusted at Oulaymatou's scheme: 'She waits for you to get married in order to throw herself at him. What a spectacle! Her attitude is unworthy of a woman of this century. Women should unite.' (*UCE*, p. 205). In the absence of such female solidarity what hope is there for a change in the status quo of male domination, and what does this entail for the future of the institution of the family, marriage and society as a whole?

Our analysis of the role of the mother-in-law in the process of abandonment may convey the impression that the primary culprit here is the woman herself. However, the fact is that Mariama Bâ sees the vanity, lust and fickle-mindedness of the male as the greater decisive factor in this process. The novelist clearly sets the limits of the influence of the woman in the process without totally dismissing its negative effects. This sense of balance accounts for the writer's ability to penetrate beneath the surface reality of women and society to present the issue in all its complexity. Yaye

Khady may have set out to chase Mireille away, but it is really Ousmane who ultimately drives her insane and leads her to commit an act designed to be a final solution to her woes. Ousmane fails miserably to balance his loyalty to a scheming selfish mother with his own responsibilities as husband and partner of a woman in need of help in a new cultural environment. He becomes a prisoner and panders to the excesses of a value system whose distorted principles the so-called enlightened people of his generation are supposed to re-evaluate in the light of current realities and exigencies. Consequently, he gets caught in a web of distortion, deception and confusion which he adamantly, but clumsily, insists on rationalizing in the name of what his friends and contemporaries such as Lamine and Boly see as false négritude. His transformation from a hardworking youth full of respect, love and devotion to his parents and girlfriend, to a vain confused young man with distorted socio-cultural values is a result of this failure. Rejected by Oulaymatou, he turns to Mireille for social and personal validation; challenged by Mireille to be responsible, he seeks escape in Oulaymatou who panders to his vanity and who now represents Africa and African culture in his eyes:

> 'Oulaymatou, double symbol in my life!' 'Symbol of the black woman' who it was his duty to liberate, 'symbol of Africa' one of whose 'enlightened sons' he was. In his mind, Oulaymatou was confused with Africa, 'an Africa to be reinstalled in her prerogatives, an Africa to be promoted.' (*UCE*, p. 225)

This sense of 'mission libératrice' becomes the spin that further turns Ousmane's mind and energy away from his obligations to his wife and son.

In both novels, Mariama Bâ examines the issue of intercaste, intercultural and interracial marriage and relationships, and she raises questions on whose satisfactory resolution will depend the stability and viability of much of the moral, political, social, economic and cultural fabric of her society. This issue is increasingly becoming a focal point for a number of African artists concerned about the nature and implications of personal and social relationships within and between societies in Africa, in particular.[4] This is the case with a number of recent African films.[5]

Although Mariama Bâ does not look at the currently topical issue of female excision and infibulation in these novels, her concern with the general issue of inequality puts her in the mainstream, if not the forefront, of contemporary feminine and African thought.

In spite of awesome odds, her heroines are champions of change and justice and they inspire other women and people to live and carry on.

This affirmative attitude toward life that the novelist invests in her heroines and that she wants to inspire in all women is conveyed in a language and form that have few parallels in African literature. One of the distinguishing features of Mariama Bâ's language is its poetic majesty which effortlessly expresses the emotion and thoughts of her characters in ways that could come only from the imagination of an accomplished woman artist. The novelist is at her best in those instances when she takes us deep into the mind and feelings of mothers disappointed with the choice of mate of their offsprings, of mothers and other women scheming to undermine one another, of mothers on the joys, pains and challenges of motherhood, of women confiding in other women, of women concerned with the political and economic health of society, and of men trapped in a quagmire of vanity, lust and deception.

Mariama Bâ's use of the letter form is unparalleled in its method and system in African literature. *Une si longue lettre* is entirely in the form of a letter while *Un chant ecarlate* makes use of intermittent letters as part of the narrative technique. Letters are used to continue the love affair between Ousmane and Mireille and at the same time to give an account of socio-political activities and information. Letters announce the marriage of Ousmane and Mireille to their respective parents, and it is an anonymous letter that exposes Ousmane's deception to Mireille. In *Une si longue lettre*, the novelist even uses the technique of a letter within a letter, as is the case when Aissatou writes Mawdo to inform him of her decision to leave. Such refined use of the epistolary form invites appropriate comparison with the recently acclaimed epistolary novel of Alice Walker, *The Color Purple*.[6]

Culture, argues Léopold Senghor, is the bedrock of development. Culture, says Ngugi wa Thiong'o, is much more than just folklore. It encompasses the entire spectrum of relations and activities in any given society. Consequently, any movement in or of society must have its feet firmly rooted in healthy cultural grounds if it is to be of any lasting and meaningful value to the welfare of individuals and society at large. And a healthy culture, in Ngugi's terms, is a culture of equality, a culture free of all forms of exploitation and, above all, a culture rooted in the true traditions of the people. In *Une si longue lettre* and *Un chant ecarlate*, Mariama Bâ uses the strength, the maturity and finesse of her imagination and artistry to reinforce this fundamental notion of culture and society. In her work, technique is combined with a sharp sense of human and social detail to capture the soulbeat of a society in the midst of a historic effort to balance its weakness and strength for a healthier future. Too bad that this female visionary left this world after writing us only one long letter and singing a beautiful song for all.[7]

NOTES

1. Mariama Bâ, *Une si longue lettre*, Dakar, Nouvelles Editions Africaines (NEA), 1980. Translated into English by Modupe Thomas as *So Long a Letter*, London, Heinemann, 1981; Ibadan, New Horn, 1982; London, Virago, 1982.
2. Mariama Bâ, *Un chant ecarlate*, Dakar, NEA, 1981.
3. All translations in this article are by the author.
4. Cf. Aminata Sow-Fall, *Le revenant*, Dakar, NEA, 1976; *La grève des battu*, Dakar, NEA, 1979; *L'appel de arènes*, Dakar, NEA, 1982; also the fictional works of Ama Ata Aidoo, and Buchi Emecheta. In non-fiction, note Awa Thiam, *La parole aux négresses*, Paris, Denoel/ Gonthier, 1978, and Ken Bugul, *Le baobab fou*, Dakar, NEA, 1982.
5. Cf. Ben Diogoye Beye, *Sey Seyeti (Un homme des femmes)*, 1979; Kramo Lancine Fadika, *Djelli*, 1980 and Kwaw Ansah, *Love Brewed In The African Pot*, 1981.
6. Alice Walker, *The Color Purple*, New York, Harcourt Brace Jovanovich, 1982.
7. Mariama Bâ passed away in August 1981 in Dakar, Senegal.

Dreams of a Common Language: Nadine Gordimer's *July's People*

Jennifer Gordon

Although Nadine Gordimer's *July's People* is primarily about the racial problems and future of South Africa, it is threaded with an important 'language' theme. Against the setting of a black takeover of South Africa, sometime in the near future, Gordimer examines, in terms of their communication, relations between a white couple, Bam and Maureen Smales, their black servant July, and the people in July's village where the Smales are hiding with their children. Through revealing presentations of the language of Bam and Maureen, Bam and July, Maureen and July, and other characters, meticulous portrayal of subtle changes in language during the course of these relationships, and realistic discussion of the power and limitations of language, Gordimer shows that the creation of a 'common language' will be necessary before any true understanding can develop between individuals in South Africa.

Of all the language relationships described in the book, Bam and Maureen's should logically be the most successful, consisting as it does of the only two adult, white, native English-speakers in the village. However, the rapid deterioration of the Smales's marriage is preceded by their growing inability to communicate verbally. At the beginning, when they have just arrived in the village, 'there was the constant subliminal feeling between him and her that they must discuss, *talk*',[1] an urge left over from their earlier life. After a while in their new circumstances, however, '[t]here were many silences between them, when each waited for the other to say what might have to be said' (p. 37), and their communication is limited to trivial discussions that avoid the questions of survival and the future. A little later, Bam realizes that '[i]t had become impossible to talk about what was happening, back there' (p. 89).

The radio, their only link with the outside world and their former existence, takes on increasing significance in their lives, even as its censorship and the eventual removal of the 'white' station from the airwaves loosen their grip on what was once reality and force them to transfer their attention to the situation at hand.

As the Smales's old expectations about each other and the world are broken down, the difficulty they have in communicating increases. Outside of their structured white world Bam is forced to see his wife and himself in a different light, and finds he 'did not know to whom to speak . . . when he spoke to her. "Maureen". "His wife". The daughter of the nice old fellow who had worked under-ground all his life . . . The girl in leotards teaching modern dance to blacks at night class . . . The other half in collusion . . . Her. Not "Maureen". Not "his wife" ' (pp. 104–5). It is as if he cannot talk to Maureen without assigning her a role, and when the old roles are no longer applicable he cannot talk to her at all. When Maureen cannot be labelled anything but 'her', she falls outside the range of Bam's language, designed as it is for comfortable communication only in their suburban marriage.

In the same way that Bam sees Maureen differently, she must confront *him* apart from his position as father and husband. Instead of concentrating on this change, as Bam chose to do, she works on the greater problems of communication with July and the other black people, distancing herself from her husband in the process. She seems to realize that the essential language problem lies outside of their marriage, and that to survive she must focus on the larger situation. The more she does this, the further behind she leaves Bam who is stuck fighting to use a now worthless language to save their almost worthless union. Even when he comes to a slightly better comprehension of the reality of their situation, he is unable to express his discovery: 'He struggled hopelessly for words that were not phrases from back there, words that would make the truth that must be forming here, out of the blacks, out of themselves . . . But the words would not come . . . The words were not there; his mind, his anger had no grip' (p. 127). The Smales's relationship is ultimately a failure because Bam is unable to adapt his language to fit their new situation, and communication between him and Maureen disappears as a result.

Since Bam is unable to communicate with Maureen, a white woman and his wife to boot, it is scarcely surprising that he fails completely in his attempts to use language with blacks. In truth, he does not even try to talk with more than two or three villagers, and all of those, men: he and Martha, July's wife, are never so much as seen together, much less do they engage in conversation. His verbal relations with the three blacks he does contact – July, the young man Daniel, and the chief – are strained at best. The most important indication of his inability to communicate is his failure to understand July even after fifteen years with him: 'Bam often irritated [July] . . . by a quick answer that made it clear, out of sheer misunderstanding, the black man's English was too poor to speak his mind' (p. 97).

In this respect, Maureen is often compared very favourably with Bam. The history of her verbal contact with July and eventually with Martha and other blacks shows a much greater desire and ability to cross language boundaries than that of her husband. She communicates with Martha and the other village women as best she can, using Afrikaans and body language; she smiles at the chief in order to open a channel between them; and, most importantly, she is serious (at least by her own standards) in her attempts to reach July through words. She is very careful not to insult him, as Bam does, by failing to comprehend his broken English: when she didn't understand him 'it was her practice to give some noncommittal sign or sound, counting on avoiding the wrong response by waiting to read back his meaning from the context of what he said next' (p. 97), and she tries to address him as an equal, especially after she realizes how dependent she is on him in the village. Blinded by her early impression of their conversations as successful, balanced exchanges, she does not realize how limited their communication is until they begin to argue about issues outside the domain of the master–servant relationship. It is only then that she sees that 'they could assume comprehension between them only if she kept away from even the most commonplace of abstractions; his was the English learned in kitchens, factories and mines. It was based on orders and responses, not the exchange of ideas and feelings.' (p. 96).

During an argument that starts over July's possession of the Smales's car keys and moves quickly on to the much greater issues of trust and equality, Maureen becomes angry and gives up the cool, rational, 'liberal' tone that she usually uses with July. When, in her frustration, she brings up the issue of his 'town woman', Ellen, 'they stepped across fifteen years of no-man's land; her words shoved them and they were together' (p. 72).

Despite his surprise at her use of this previously unmentioned knowledge, July refuses the opportunity to answer her as an equal in anger, carefully maintaining the role of a 'servant [who] replied uninterestedly to a dutiful inquiry on the part of the good madam who knows better than to expose herself to an answer from the real facts of his life' (p. 72). At this point, the balance of verbal power, and the balance of power in their relationship, shift. No longer does July play the part of the servant through necessity; he can assume the role when it is advantageous to him. No longer can Maureen speak to July as an equal only when it is convenient; she must recognize that his status does not depend on her whims or good will. The climax of this new phase is reached at the very end of the book, when Maureen confronts July with the simultaneous disappearance of the Smales's gun and Daniel. Unhappy with his role, and remembering what he had been forced to pretend to and betray in the past as part of his servant's position, July 'began to talk at her in his own language, his face flickering powerfully . . . She understood although she knew no word. Understood everything: what he had had to be, how she had covered up to herself for him, in order for him to be her idea of him' (p. 152). Unfortunately, this symbolic bilingualism does not last, both because what Maureen learns is too painful and because years of conditioning have made the concept of a 'common language' that lasts more than a few minutes impossible between a white and a black in South Africa.

Although the use of language on a broad scale is the major communication theme in this book, subtle changes in language are also very important. July, for one, is masterful at slight manipulations of English to achieve a desired effect, altering the sophistication of his syntax and vocabulary to fit the situation. While playing servant and caretaker, he lapses into pidgin talk ('Is coming plenty rain . . . is nice easy, isn't it? You see, your father he make everyone-everyone to be pleased' [p. 63]) that contrasts with his still stilted, but more dignified, normal English speech ('It's not the keys for your kitchen. Fifteen years I'm work for your kitchen, your house, because my wife, my children, I must work for them' [p. 72]). Another technique that he uses effectively is simulated misunderstanding, when he pretends to have misheard demeaning statements or accusations from white people. These tactics work quite well, and they need to – they are his only advantage when speaking English.

In this same category of 'subtle change' falls the issue of naming and how names evolve over time. The two most important examples of this are Bam, who moves from 'Bam' to 'my husband' to 'that man' in Maureen's mind as she distances herself from him; and July, who is called by his African name Mwawate at the end of the book. This conversion reflects his very important shift in position from a black servant judged by white people in English, to a black man judged by black people in his own language.

Another example of the importance of naming is the running argument between the Smaleses and July over the latter's use of the word 'master'. 'He used to have the habit of knocking at a door, asking, The master he say I can come in?, and they had tried to train him to drop the "master" for the ubiquitously respectful "sir"' (p. 52). Semantics are the issue here: the word 'master' offends the ears of the Smaleses, connoting as it does the old master–slave arrangement; they feel the word 'sir' better reflects their situation. For July, Bam *is* the master, and to call him 'sir' will not change their relationship at all. 'How many times, back there, had Maureen and Bam tried to get him to drop the Simon Legree term, but he wouldn't, couldn't, as if there were no term to replace it, none that would express exactly what the relationship\between Bam and him was, for him' (p. 111). The Smaleses believe that by changing names they can somehow change status, and they present their refusal to use the word 'master' as evidence of their liberalism: in desperation, Maureen says to July, ' "*The master.* Bam's not your master. Why do you pretend? Nobody's ever thought of you as anything but a grown man" ' (p. 71). July, for his part, sees the situation differently, sees himself as 'their boy', and refuses to allow the white people to claim anything else: 'You tell everybody you trust your good boy. You are good madam, you got good boy' (p. 70). Their entire relationship is summed up by July as 'Fifteen years/your boy/you satisfy' (p. 98), and nothing that Maureen or anyone else can say will change his perception, which is so unlike the Smales's. This is where language fails. Despite their many powers, words cannot perform the miracle of conversion that Bam and Maureen are looking for without a much greater change from outside.

There are other situations in the book where words fail or are misused. Often, formulas take the place of any true exchange of feeling: when the Smaleses meet the chief, for instance, he murmurs 'deeply and hastily over a formula of greeting (they wouldn't understand, anyway) whose tone contradicted, authoritatively, any welcome or acceptance' (p. 111), and for July, there was 'the servant's formula, attuned to catch the echo of the master's concern, to remove combat and conflict tactfully, fatalistically, in mission-classroom phrases, to the neutrality of divine will' (pp. 94–5). Even when he appears to be communicating on a deeper level with white people, as in his conversations with Maureen, the words eventually break down and reveal themselves for what they have been all along – a train of formulas, said with feeling but without deep thought, satisfactory and useful between servant and master, but completely inadequate for any deeper relationship. In fact, most of the interpersonal communication in this book can be pared down to a series of pre-prepared formulas (husband to wife, parent to child, black to white), and it is only when the participants step outside these set roles that they actually communicate.

Another common failure is language in translation. From July's inept renderings of the chief's speech (made all the more ironic by the chief's English-speaking ability revealed later), to Maureen's book *I promessi sposi* which 'was translated from the Italian but would not translate to the kind of comprehension she was able to provide now' (pp. 138–9), to the constant translations in South African life made necessary by the linguistic separation of the races (and the mutations, strictly constructed to preserve the status quo, that come from this situation, like 'the bastard *lingua franca* of the mines, whose vocabulary was limited to orders given by whites and responses made by blacks', [p. 45]; much is lost when words in one language are converted to another. One of the most devastating examples of the dangers of translation is seen when Maureen finally stops simplifying her language for July and lets loose a tirade: 'she didn't know . . . if he understood the words; she dropped fifteen years of the habit of translation into very simple, concrete vocabulary. If she had never before used the word 'dignity' to him it was not because she didn't think he understood the concept, didn't have any – it was only the term itself that might be beyond his grasp of the language' (p. 72). If translating means that such grave ommissions are necessary, then clearly translation is a large impediment to real communication.

Despite the pessimism of much of Gordimer's portrayal, there *are* hints in the book that language and communication can succeed in the right circumstances. First, there is frequent emphasis on the potential power of words, best illustrated when Bam, speaking to July after the disappearance of their car, 'stepped through a minefield of words before he chose what to say' (p. 53). Then there is the example of the children, who pick up the essentials of the black language quickly and easily. The 'deep and secret' (p. 157) friendship of Gina, the Smales's daughter, and Nyiko, a village girl, is one instance of this; another is the body language that Victor, the Smales's son, has picked up by the end of the book, when he 'is seen to clap his hands, sticky with mealie *pap*, softly, gravely together and bob obeisance, receiving the gift with cupped palms' (p. 157); both suggest hope of a common language for future generations. Finally, there is Maureen's already mentioned moment of bilingualism, which suggests, however briefly, that a temporary language revolution is a possibility even in the present.

It is obvious, then, that Gordimer believes in major change through words. However, although she is hopeful, she is careful to keep language's limitations in mind. When forced into set formulas, as it often is in black–white and male–female relations; when translated or taken out of context, as it must always be for someone speaking, hearing, or reading what is not their own language; when used as a screen or to control someone else; language fails to live up to its potential. In the end, Gordimer shows true communication in South Africa to be a very rare occurence, a small island of properly used words surrounded by a sea of rigid formulas, inaccurate translations, intentional misunderstandings, and useless word games. When this is the case, when the current language proves itself to be as inadequate to the South African situation as English seems to be, it is time to do one of two things: either change the situation to fit the useless language (as the whites have tried to do for so long), or change the language itself. At that point, the only real solution is a revolution, for, as the West Indian poet Derek Walcott wrote, 'To change your language you must change your life.'

NOTES

1. Nadine Gordimer, *July's People*, London, Penguin Books, 1981, p. 35. All subsequent quotations are from this edition.

Ama Ata Aidoo and the Oral Tradition: A Paradox of Form and Substance

Arlene Elder

In 1967, the Ghanaian writer, Ama Ata Aidoo asserted:

> I totally disagree with people who feel that oral literature is one stage in the development of man's artistic genius. To me it's an end in itself . . .
>   We cannot tell our stories maybe with the same expertise as our forefathers. But to me, all the art of the speaking voice could be brought back so easily. We are not that far from our traditions.[1]

This comment has served readers well in clarifying Aidoo's aesthetic and cultural concerns and providing a key to her style. Certainly, her plays, *The Dilemma of a Ghost* (1965) and *Anowa* (1969), and collection of short stories, *No Sweetness Here* (1972) all demonstrate her allegiance to oral performance and her skilful re-creation of the traditional unity of performer and audience.

Her most recent work, *Our Sister Killjoy or Reflections from a Black-eyed Squint* (1979),[2] is most interesting, however, because, paradoxically, it utilizes the very devices of Ghanaian oral literature to suggest that colonialism has fractured African society so severely that art is no longer both 'a form of aesthetic expression and a mode of communication', solidly rooted in 'underlying social, cultural and religious values', as J.H. Kwabena Nketia describes traditional drama.[3] Instead, the contemporary African artist, in Aidoo's view, is unsure of, even rebuffed by, his audience. His attempts at communal expression are stifled; his fate, ironically, is like that of his Western counterpart: to speak in isolation, most often in defiance and frustration. It is nothing less than a *tour de force* that Aidoo successfully employs traditional oral techniques to present us with such a non-traditional conclusion.

The book jacket announces that *Our Sister Killjoy* is a novel, but at first glance, it appears to be a *mélange* of fictional episodes in both prose and verse mixed with sections of political speculation and social criticism. The book is divided into four parts: 'Into A Bad Dream', 'The Plums', 'From Our Sister Killjoy', and 'A Love Letter'. Briefly, the story is of 'our Sister', Sissie, who is selected by officials in Ghana to accompany other young Africans to a youth hostel in Germany. There, she develops a troubling relationship with a discontented and lonely German housewife and learns something about connections between women and, particularly, about her own predicament as an African woman. She then travels to London and comes face-to-face with others like herself who had left Africa for the promises of Western education. In the end, she returns to Africa, but only after arguing with her compatriots and alienating her lover because of her outspoken political beliefs.

Aidoo tells this story in the third-person, using the omniscient narrator common to many Western novels, but the narrative proper does not begin until page 8. Preceding the story are several pages of curiously spaced, conversational observations about neo-colonial, 'moderate' blacks and, 'academic-pseudo-intellectuals' (p. 6). Page 6 is only three-quarters filled with prose; pages 5 and 7 are shaped like poems; and pages 3 and 4 consist of only one line apiece.

In addition to this unusual typography, the feature that suggests that Aidoo has something other than the conventional novel in mind is the conversational nature of these passages. She begins with the reassurance, 'Things are working out' (p. 3), as though the reader already knows what these 'Things' are. This casual, imprecise beginning establishes a dynamic between reader and writer essential to Aidoo's overall goal.

First, as every good story-teller must, she whets her reader's curiosity to discover what has been happening to her speaker, what it is that might be in doubt of 'working out'. Second, by beginning in the middle of the action, she establishes a bond of prior acquaintanceship with her reader. When the narrator then calls him, 'my brother' (p. 7), he is transformed from a stranger, a distant reader of a novel on a cold, printed page, interested privately in a good story, perhaps, into a member of her community involved in the very situation confronting the main character. Moreover, the style in these first pages tends toward the epistolary, a technique she will make explicit in the fourth section, thus enhancing the intimacy between writer and reader, between speaker and listener. In a very real sense, because Aidoo has defined her audience so carefully, both by the conversational style and by the designation, 'my brother', we, as readers, become participants and, at least temporarily, part of her society, confronting the dilemmas of one of our own kind whose experiences and decisions hold meaning for our own lives. Such is the traditional dynamic between the African poet and his audience.

Aidoo enhances this effect by shaping her narrative with other traditional techniques. Throughout the story, for example, there are passages written in poetic form, like the songs interspersed throughout the oral performance of a folk tale. 'In the evenings', reports Okechukwu Mezu in *African Writers on African Writing*,

> When children gather to listen to stories, yarns and fairy-tales from their grandparents, they listen to pieces interspersed with rhymes, lyrics and choruses . . . One of the most interesting aspects of traditional African civilization is the unity of the art forms.[4]

In form and substance, Aidoo's verse in this book most resembles the type of traditional poetry described by Kofi Antubam in *Ghana's Heritage of Culture* as 'Abentia Munsem', that is, very short verses that:

> often are reminders to chiefs of a certain calamity that had befallen their state or community in the past. Sometimes, too, they warn them of either their responsibilities as head of their state or first member of the royal family. Where no trouble has come in the way of a state or community, its chief ABENTIA player serves as the secret guide of his master, and forewarns him when he is about to meet some trouble and fall into the hands of his enemies.[5]

African writers rooted in their traditions strive for an integration of established and changing social customs and combine, in critic Lloyd Brown's words, 'a sense of permanence with a process of continual change.'[6] Like the verses of the Abentia player of old, Aidoo's songs confront her listeners with their sense of political calamity, in this instance, colonialism, but her awareness of historical change demands that they be intended as warnings for the common people, her 'brothers', not the neo-colonial heads of state whom she mistrusts.

An example of this poetry occurs in the second section, 'The Plums', when Sissie is recounting her tour of Upper Volta to her new German friend, Marija. 'Was Upper Wolta also beautiful' Marija asks:

She did not know she thought so then.
She was to know.

The bible talks of
Wilderness
Take your eyes to see
Upper Volta, my brother –
Dry land. Thorn trees. Stones.

The road from the Ghana border to
Ouagadougou was
Out-of-sight!

The French, with
Characteristic contempt and
Almost
Childish sense of
Perfidy had
A long time ago, tarred two
Narrow
Strips of earth for motor vehicles.
Each wide enough for
One tyre. (p. 54).

A prose section follows, recounting a near disaster occurring to
three travellers as a result of the shoddy paving of the road and
highlighting the French indifference to such accidents. Then, the
verse continues:

A sickening familiar tale.
Poor Upper Volta too.

There are
Richer, much
Richer countries on this continent
Where
Graver national problems
Stay
Unseen while
Big men live their
Big lives
Within . . . (p. 55).

The first section of the book, 'Into A Bad Dream', is connected to
'The Plums' by three pages containing one word each: 'Where',
'When', 'How' (pp. 14–16). These words are not presented as questions, but as statements. They are the equivalent of the narrator
saying something like: 'Now, I will tell you *where* Sissy went, *when*
she returned, and *how* her time in Europe progressed.' Therefore,

they serve as a bridge in the narrative and are not really conversational; rather, they are like subject headings in a notebook.

Nevertheless, almost immediately, she re-establishes the oral quality of her narrative by introducing first, a poetic passage inspired by Sissie's visiting a German castle and reflecting on the misuse of power by the nobility and secondly, another moving prose vignette about the plight of some naive Asians, ignorant of the discrimination in the West against people with dark skin. Such alternation of prose features with poetic narrative and reflection is the pattern of the first three sections of the work and illustrates Aidoo's adherence to the similar structure of African oral performance. As Mezu observes, 'side by side with [the] unity of the art forms is the element of repetition . . . a litany that says the same thing in various ways . . .'[7]

The third section, 'From Our Sister Killjoy', serves a dual purpose: to expose the self-delusion and dishonesty of the 'been-tos' and to characterize Sissie as perceiving the discrepancies between what she has been told of the life of Africans abroad and what she actually confronts in England: 'Sissie bled as she tried to take the scene in. The more people she talked to, the less she understood' (p. 85). When she sees again and again the pitiful condition of the Africans in London, whatever their claims or expectations, her first reaction is to weep and then to rage. Aidoo uses the third-person narrator to judge Sissie's growth at various points in the book, for one way to look at this novel is as a story of maturation. 'Our poor sister,' the narrator laments,

> So touchingly naive then . . .
> She wondered why they never told the truth of their travels at home.
> Not knowing that if they were to keep on being something in their own eyes, then they could not tell the truth to their own selves or to anyone else (p. 89).

'So when they eventually went back home as "been-tos",' like Ato of the author's first play, they returned 'the ghosts of the humans that they used to be . . .' (p. 89).

This third section ends with the satiric episode of Sissie's meeting with a typical 'been-to', Kunle. Their disagreement about a current news item, the first heart transplants, demonstrates Aidoo's ability to satirize and identify a prominent figure she feels worthy of criticism without actually naming him, a skill valued in traditional oral performance. In *Yes and No, the Intimate Folklore of Africa*, Alta Jablow points out that in oral performance:

Often, in addition to the traditional stories and legends, topical items are recounted though disguised as fiction with sly humor and sarcasm. The pretentious, the wily and dishonest are thus often criticized publicly. If the talent of the narrator is such that the personalities involved can be recognized, though he is avoiding specific reference to them, so much the better.[8]

After Sissie and Kunle's disagreement, in which it is revealed that the first hearts transplanted were from Coloured South Africans to white South Africans, the narrator remarks:

That was some years
Before
A colleague described
The Christian Doctor's nth triumph as being
        'Dangerously close to outright
        experimentation.'
. . . .
Meanwhile
One or two more
Idealistic
Young
Refugees
Have gone totally
Mad – or got themselves killed on
the Zambezi.
The Christian Doctor has
Taken a couple of press pictures
In the company of a
Movie Queen

Divorced
Mrs. Christian Doctor

Acquired another
Mrs. Christian Doctor
and a couple of rand
Millions
Effected quite a few more
Heart transplantations.
He is the only one
Who seems
Now to be doing well;
The rest?
A veritable catalogue of
Death and just plain
Heartbreak (pp. 97, 102).

The futility of the 'been-tos' like Kunle who support whatever they find in the West, heart transplants, for instance, no matter how barbaric such 'advances' may actually be, and the frequently dashed dreams of those awaiting their return are emphasized by Kunle's mother's letter to him at the end of the third part.

The device of the epistle is extended in the concluding section, 'A Love Letter'. The form here – first-person narration of a letter Sissie is writing on her plane back to Africa – reinforces the conversational emphasis of the preceding chapters and allows us an even greater intimacy with Aidoo's heroine through direct contact with her innermost thoughts expressed in her own voice. Appropriately, it is here in her own words that Sissie expresses her own and, no doubt, Aidoo's reservations about language and the possibility of communication. Such questioning raises the very serious issue of the possibility of traditional art in a neo-colonial society. 'First of all, there is this language!', she begins in complaint, 'This language . . . so far, I have only been able to use a language that enslaved me, and therefore, the messengers of my mind always come shackled . . .' (p. 112). Language, then, like everything else she discovers on her odyssey, carries political overtones which affect individuals as well as societies. Her letter is to a man she still loves but who considers her too politically radical for him and, like the heroine of Aidoo's second play, *Anowa*, not womanly enough. He has decided to remain in London, not return to Africa.

Sissie reads and rereads the letter, like the reader, acquainting herself with her new ideas and refining her new perceptions. If the story had ended here, the book's reliance on traditional oral performance would have been in keeping with Aidoo's earlier works. As listeners, we would have been drawn into the action more intimately with each succeeding section and, possibly, would have been affected like the traditional audience to the point that the story would have reflected and perpetuated our own moral and cultural values. However, most of the fictional 'brothers' Sissie meets do not share her concern about selling themselves for the fool's gold of the West, thus betraying Africa; and we, her readers in the West can only be her 'brothers' ideologically, at best, not culturally. The distancing technique Aidoo uses at the end of the fourth section, which will be discussed below, suggests that she realizes the isolating effect that colonialism has brought to the storyteller and the resulting change in the power of his art.

Analyzing the historical context of African poetry, Okechukwu Mezu explains:

> African traditional poetry can . . . be described as a collective experi-
> ence initiated by an individual in a group and shared by the rest. It is a
> conscious and finalistic attempt to verbalize, vocalize or orchestrate
> notions, themes and/or events for enjoyment, parody, or veneration
> with a view to artistic recreation, group catharsis or supernatural
> contemplation.[9]

Modern African poetry – Mezu is particularly concerned with
revolutionary poetry – like Western poetry, however, is personal:

> From a group catharsis, modern African poetry became an experiment
> in self-exorcism. Because he can no longer speak to his people, the
> modern African poet has chosen to sing, chant, shout, be angry, rave,
> curse, condemn and praise when occasion demands it in the interests of
> his people.[10]

Unlike the audience for whom the revolutionary poet writes,
Sissie's 'brothers' do not seem to want to overthrow their psychological and political 'bosses' (p. 6). All the compatriots she meets in
London offer her multiple rationalizations as to why they should
remain there. She knows that even the man she loves would react
to her letter by saying:

> There you go again, Sissie, you are so serious (p. 112);
> Dear Lord, all you radicals make me sick. How oversensitive do you
> people want to be? (p. 113);

and:

> There goes Sissie again. Forever carrying Africa's problems on her
> shoulders as though they have paid her to do it (p. 118).

She realizes he might not even be listening to her and has to ask him
in Swahili, 'Unasika, Mpenzi Wangu?', which is 'Are you listening,
my love?' (p. 115)

Finally, she decides not to mail the letter. The last few pages of
this section return to the voice of the third-person narrator,
distancing us from Sissie, as she feels herself distanced from all
but the beautiful continent of Africa itself, which inspires and
nourishes her: '. . . she was back in Africa. And that felt like fresh
wild honey on the tongue . . .' (p. 133).

Colonialism has broken the circle of singer and listener, orator
and audience. Sissie learns that she cannot speak to her 'brothers'
in any tongue: 'I hadn't been aware that I was making a speech',

she remembers a particularly unpleasant confrontation with them: 'when I paused the silence made itself heard.' (p. 130) Nor can she speak for them: 'Listen, Sister. You cannot make these blanket statements.', they inform her (p. 126).

In the end, she speaks only to and for herself:

> 'Oh, Africa. Crazy old continent . . .'
> Sissie wondered whether she had spoken aloud to herself. The occupant of the next seat probably thought she was crazy. Then she decided she didn't care anyway (pp. 133–4).

Sissie's travels have led to her growth in understanding and self-confidence, but unlike her predecessors, the Abentia players of old, she is isolated, without an audience, without a community of shared values.

And so, in search of unity of meaning, at least, we circle back with the narrator's voice to the first statements in the work and realize that, despite her pessimism, as embodied in Sissie's failure to send the letter and her sense of isolation and defiance, Aidoo does not despair. 'Things are working out', the narrator has promised,

> towards their dazzling conclusions . . .
>
> . . . so it is neither here nor there,
> what ticky-tackies we have
> saddled and surrounded ourselves with,
> blocked our views,
> cluttered our brains (pp. 3–5).

The narrator, always superior to Sissie in understanding, provides structural unity for the narrative and, at the same time, establishes Aidoo's paradoxical role as an artist attempting to continue the moral function of the communal oral performer in an individualistic, materialistic present. While, like Africa itself, art, culture, morality continue, despite attacks on them, Aidoo has demonstrated that the communication of these verities has become increasingly difficult. The artist's unifying and strengthening role is diminished, and the bond between singer and audience is broken. One may revitalize the forms of traditional culture as Aidoo demonstrates so skilfully in all of her work, but history has guaranteed that the substance, the ethical bond between artist and audience, will probably never return.

NOTES

1. Ama Ata Aidoo in an interview by Maxine McGregor in Cosmo Pieterse and Dennis Duerden (eds), *African Writers Talking, a Collection of Radio Interviews*, New York, Africana Publishing Company, 1972, pp. 23,24.
2. Ama Ata Aidoo, *Our Sister Killjoy or Reflections from a Black-eyed Squint*, New York, Nok Publishers, 1979, p. 6. Hereafter, quotations are from this edition, unless otherwise noted.
3. J.H. Kwabena Nketia, *Music, Dance and Drama, a Review of the Performance Arts in Ghana*, Legon, Institute of African Studies, 1965, p. 36.
4. S. Okechukwu Mezu, 'Poetry and Revolution in Modern Africa', in G.D. Killam (ed.), *African Writers on African Writing*, London, Heinemann, 1973, pp. 91–108, pp. 92–3.
5. Kofi Antubam, *Ghana's Heritage of Culture*, Leipzig, Koehler & Amelang, 1963, p. 139.
6. Lloyd W. Brown, *Women Writers in Black Africa*, Westport, Conn., Greenwood Press, 1981, p. 99.
7. Mezu, 'Poetry and Revolution', pp. 93, 94.
8. Alta Jablow, *Yes and No, the Intimate Folklore of Africa*, New York, Horizon Press, 1961, p. 30.
9. Brown, *Women Writers*, p. 85.
10. Mezu, 'Poetry and Revolution', p. 95.
11. ibid., 95–6.

Images of Woman in Wole Soyinka's Work

Sylvia Bryan

Soyinka's work evinces no preoccupation with woman's domestic roles as wife and mother although in *Idanre and Other Poems* he presents the traditional image of woman as the conduit and sustainer of life. His drama and novels therefore contain scarcely any domestic scenes such as are found in Chinua Achebe's novels, Ayi Kwei Armah's *The Beautyful Ones Are Not Yet Born* and *Fragments* or Ngugi Wa Thiong'o's *A Grain of Wheat*. Moreover, such few scenes as he presents occur in earlier works like *The Swamp Dwellers* and *Camwood on the Leaves*.[1] Later, impelled by the pressure of circumstances and his increasing concern with contemporary political developments in Nigeria, Soyinka began to see a specific public role for women, that of catalyst in revolutionary socio-political change. This is particularly evident in the portrayals of Segi in *Kongi's Harvest* and Iriyise in *Season of Anomy*.

Not unrelated to Soyinka's presentation of the political woman is the emergence of the recurring elusive siren, usually a courtesan. Although one sees some development in the characterization of this type, there is some justification for Christine Purisch's criticism of Soyinka's tendency to portray an archetypal female image, thus precluding the depiction of 'real women'.[2] Soyinka has himself stated that the primary function of woman in his work is that of symbol and essence.[3] Despite the awareness that such a function precludes a 'balanced' presentation of woman, one cannot but question its validity, especially when it dictates a minor economic role for his women as viewed against the background of the major role of, for example, the Yoruba woman in Nigerian national economic life. (The cynic might observe that in *Opera Wonyosi* Soyinka repairs this picture in the portrayal of the amoral, rapacious De Madam and her daughter Polly.)

With regard to Soyinka's portrayal of woman as political activist, there are precedents both in Yoruba legend and Nigerian politics of the pre-independence era. According to Yoruba myth, Moremi, a Yoruba priestess, sacrificed her son Oberogbo to the Esumerin stream and underwent captivity by the Igbos in order to deliver Ife from constant attack by Igbo marauders.[4] On the advice of the spirit of the stream she allowed herself to be captured by a group of Igbos. Her beauty and deportment won her the love of the king who took her as one of his wives. Utilizing this position, she learned the secret of the Igbo's mastery of the Yoruba in battle. After escaping from the community she revealed this secret to the Yoruba, enabling them to defeat the next set of marauders. In fulfilment of her promise, she sacrificed her only child, Olurogbo, to the stream.

In the politics of modern Nigeria, the now deceased Mrs Funmilayo Ransome-Kuti*, Soyinka's aunt, was a pioneer. As a foundation member of the Nigerian National Democratic Party, Kuti waged a relentless campaign to terminate British rule until Nigeria gained its independence in 1960.[5] Within Nigeria, her struggles with local authorities to protect the rights of women, especially with regard to their market trade, culminated in the exile of the Alake of Abeokuta in 1948. Subsequent repercussions on the administration of Local Councils throughout Nigeria ensured the initiation of fundamental reforms affecting the administration of markets.[6]

Another fact which we will consider in reading the characters of Segi and Iriyise is Soyinka's growing sympathy for a socialist ideology.[7] Penda, a prostitute in Sembène Ousmane's *God's Bits of Wood*, is probably the predecessor of Soyinka's two courtesan political activists. An examination of the conceptual relationship between both characters, the awareness that by the time Soyinka wrote *Season of Anomy* he had expressed strong socialist views and that Ousmane is an avowed socialist writer whose novel and commitment to socialism preceded Soyinka's, present a perspective from which to examine the woman as political rebel in Soyinka's work.

Penda, during the march of strikers to Dakar, moves to counteract both the women's fatigue and the superstition that Awa has caused to dampen the spirits of the marching women. Making a desperate last attempt to force them to move forward, she breaks a serious tribal taboo and relentlessly begins to count the women:

'One, two, three, four . . .'
'Witch!' Awa cried. 'You have no right to do that!'
'No, no! Don't count us, please!' Séni said, getting quickly to her feet.

---

*Editors' note: Soyinka treats the role of Mrs Ransome-Kuti in his autobiographical work, *Akè: The Years of Childhood*, London, Rex Collings, 1981

'We are God's bits of wood and if you count us out you will bring
misfortune; you will make us die!'[8]

Goaded by both fear and anger, the women gather their clothing,
knot their cloths around their heads and return to the road to
resume the march to Dakar. Penda's crucial role in mobilizing the
women to support the railway strike against the toubabs culminates in her becoming a martyr of the 'revolution' as she is shot in
the front line of marchers on the way to Dakar.[9]

The Soyinkan woman whose attitude and role is most similar to
Penda's is Iriyise in *Season of Anomy*. The Dentist, a Marxist-
Leninist, comments on Iriyise's importance as a symbol for the
liberation movement:

> We must acknowledge the fact – pimps, whores . . . are the familiar
> vanguard of the army of change. When the moment arrives a woman
> like Iriyise becomes for the people a Chantal, a Deborah, torch and
> standard-bearer, super mistress of universal insurgence. To abandon
> such a potential weapon in any struggle is to admit to a lack of foresight.
> Or imagination.[10]

As Ofeyi's companion and confederate in undermining and
destroying the power base of the Cartel, Iriyise sings the subver-
sive lyrics which Ofeyi composes to be presented by Zaccheus and
his Cocoa Beans orchestra.[11] As the Cocoa Princess, Iriyise presents one of Ofeyi's most vivid and highly symbolic creations
designed to expose the corruption, brutality and sheer destruc-
tiveness of the Cartel. The 'Pandora's Box' routine is particularly
apt in conveying the extent to which the Cartel has simultaneously
introduced evil into the society and unleashed the forces which are
serving to decimate the populace.[12]

Her concern for the cause manifests itself in her abandonment of
'the circuit of Ilosa's lights' for the rural village of Aiyéró. She
becomes completely immersed in the life style of the village:

> In wrapper and sash with the other women of Aiyéró, her bared limbs
> and shoulders among young shoots, Iriyise weaving fronds for the pro-
> tection of the young nursery, bringing wine to the sweating men in their
> struggle against the virgin forests . . . From merely singing praises of
> the 'cocoa complexion' . . . she could even tell a blight on the young
> shoot apart from mere scorching by the sun. Her fingers spliced
> wounded saplings with the ease of a natural healer.[13]

Expressing her preference for dancing for the workers over
making 'Personal Appearances at the homes of fat Corporation
swine', she gives a superb and zealous performance at the 'gala

night' arranged by the workers at the Shage Dam, 'the Cross River outpost of the new idea'. Iriyise impresses the reader as a politically active woman aware of the ideological base of her involvement and of what she is struggling to defeat. She emerges as not merely an accomplice to Ofeyi, her lover, as does Segi in *Kongi's Harvest*, but as a thinking person with a personal commitment. In passing, it is instructive to note that Wanja, in Ngugi's *Petals of Blood*, plays an even more catalytic role in the political and economic mobilization of the villagers of Ilmorog, in concert with Karega, Munira and Abdulla. She also organizes the women into an Ndemi-Nyakinya Group to produce crops more profitably.[14] That Wanja is the product of a socialist ideology serves to accentuate the belief that Soyinka's ideological perspective accounted for his portrayal of Iriyise.

When one compares the much earlier portrayal of Segi – *Kongi's Harvest* was published in 1965 and *Season of Anomy* in 1973 – with that of Iriyise, it becomes clear that Soyinka's conception of woman as political activist has become more positive. Segi's plans to overthrow Kongi's dictatorial regime are partly motivated by personal concerns. Her father has been detained by Kongi and faces possible execution, while she has been rebuffed by the latter who rejected or betrayed the love she once proffered.[15] To effect Kongi's overthrow, she mobilizes some 'rehabilitated' prostitutes, members of the Women's Auxiliary Corps and a number of layabouts disgruntled with Kongi's regime. She acts in concert with Daodu and the farmers he has organized. However, after Daodu wins the New Yam Segi confesses, 'It is wrong to feel so selfish, but now that my father has escaped, I wish this plan was never made'.[16] Although, when Daodu's nerve seems to fail, she courageously sends the head of her father to Kongi as a symbol of the latter's impending death, the dominant image of Segi is that of the voluptuary. This is particularly evident in the scene prior to the confrontation with Kongi where she pleads with Daodu to make love to her. Although he is insistent that their incomplete plans for overthrowing Kongi demand urgent attention, she persists:

SEGI: Come with me Daodu.
DAODU: Now? There is still much to do before you meet us at the gates.
SEGI: Come through the gates tonight. Now. I want you in me, my Spirit of Harvest.
DAODU: Don't tempt me so hard. I am swollen like prize yam under earth, but all harvest must await its season.

SEGI: There is no season for seeds bursting.
DAODU: My eyes of kernels, I have much preparation to make.
SEGI   I shall help you.
DAODU: Segi, between now and tomorrow's eve, I must somehow
         obtain some rest.
SEGI: Let me tire you a little more.
DAODU: You cannot know how weary I am . . .
SEGI: I must rejoice and you with me . . .[17]

Iriyise, on the other hand, is so engrossed in her commitment to her political task and especially to her quest for knowledge of the 'heart-beat of Aiyéró' that she can detach her romantic interests from her political concerns. Her absorption in the affairs of the village is so great that Ofeyi 'had often been afraid that her new world might indeed exclude the ecstatic aspects of their bond.'[18]

Segi and Iriyise are, however, similar in their presentation as stereotypes of the siren, though Segi is also cannibal. In the latter aspect she is part of a sisterhood with predecessors in Simi of *The Interpreters* and Rola/Madame Tortoise of *A Dance of the Forests*. Simi, Queen Ant and Queen Bee, has a fatal fascination for men. Just as drones die after fertilizing the Queen Bee and the male ants after mating with the Queen Ant, so too Egbo figuratively dies after his night with Simi. He has to seek renewal through contact with nature:

And after this, the second time, Egbo felt he was like the quarry at Abeokuta when all the granite had been blown apart and nothing but mud-waters of the rain fill the huge caverns underground . . . .
    Some balance in his life was upset and he boarded the train that Sunday afternoon feeling distinctly hollowed out, weak, nervous and apprehensive . . . He shook off sleep and took off his clothes . . . His swimming was brief . . . Egbo rose and looked around him, bathing and wondering at life, for it seemed to him that he was born again.[19]

Simi is described as the 'beast that lay in wait to swallow [Egbo]' and the latter in his relationship with her becomes 'immersed in a cannibal's reality', yet 'Egbo found his will was towards consummation, even self-destruction in the process.'[20]

Segi too is presented as 'a right cannibal of the female species' who sucks the vigour and vitality from men, leaving them 'like sugar cane pulp/Squeezed dry.' Danlola cautions Daodu against her:

Oh you have chosen to be swallowed whole
Down the oyster throat of the witch
Of night clubs. Segi! Son, she'll shave
Your skull and lubricate it in oil.[21]

Madame Tortoise/Rola, has a similarly destructive effect on men; a personification of the sex urge, she drives men to desperation by intoxicating them with an irrepressible desire for her, as do Simi, Segi and Iriyise. Her insatiable desire has made her mistress to a whole band of soldiers from whom she selects a new lover every day.[22] She destroys the lives of the Warrior and his wife when he refuses to be seduced. As Rola, she indiscriminately wrecks both young and old.

The suggestion that woman is a type of cannibal in her sexual relationship with man does not only find corollaries in nature – the bee, the ant, the praying mantis which often involuntarily eats its mate during the act of love-making – but also in fiction, as in D.H. Lawrence's portrayal of the relationship between Anton Skrebensky and Ursula Brangwen in *The Rainbow*:

> But it all contained a developing germ of death. After each contact . . . his hope of standing strong and taking her in his own strength was weakened. He felt himself a mere attribute of her.[23]

The feminist might argue that this is mere perpetuation of the negative image of woman. However, an examination of the siren image might support the interpretation that Soyinka's depiction of this aspect of woman is another illustration of his recognition of the inevitable contradictions or duality inherent in human experience, embodied most noticeably in the creative-destructive Ogun personality which informs most of his work.

Simi, Segi and Iriyise are physically beautiful, their allure captivates men, so they whimsically refuse lovers. The fascinating yet dangerous quality of the siren is conveyed in Danlola's description of Segi as a 'python coiled/In wait for rabbits'.[24] The duality of the snake image encapsulates the apparent contradictions of irresistible beauty, deception and danger of the siren. With overtones of the Fall in which woman was instrumental, Soyinka is implying that duality is an inescapable part of the human experience of which the male–female relationship is an aspect. In addition, Soyinka does suggest elsewhere that the man–woman relationship is vital to man's maturity, self-knowledge and psychic awareness. This is particularly true of Egbo's relationship with Simi. His first sexual experience with her constitutes his initiation 'into his part in the life mysteries':

> he felt a terror of the senses . . . for his body was in that instant gelled to the earth and heavens, and the pull of life from within his sensuousness he felt as the rending of heavenly vaults and upheaval in earth's core.[25]

Through the presentation of the Ofeyi–Iriyise relationship, Soyinka suggests, despite the emphasis on Iriyise's temperamental behaviour, that having plumbed the depths of the male–female relationship, one somehow attains to a deeper understanding of the meaning of life. One is never quite sure how this is achieved, but there are indications that this is partly due to mutual commitment:

> Iriyise, still, except for her eyes which followed Ofeyi's motions, and Ofeyi in the loose white wrap . . . priest and vestal in mutual admiration. And why not, thought Ofeyi? Vision is eternally of man's own creating. The woman's acceptance, her collaboration in man's vision of life results time and time again in just such periodic embodiments of earth and ideal.[26]

That woman somehow helps to hone man's sensibility to greater sensitivity and instinctive awareness is also suggested by the role of the wine girl/Oya in 'Idanre'. Although she does not comprehend the purpose of the poet/protagonist's dangerous quest, she seems to be a human anchor and a haven from the turbulent physical and psychic experience of the protagonist, the one psychic link with the living. As Oya, a symbol of quiet, beauty and order, and the antithesis of Ogun, she functions as a mother figure who guarantees security, rest and fruitfulness and provides sustenance during the most turbulent and trying times.

Soyinka therefore goes beyond the femme fatale image of, for example, Ihuoma of Elechi Amadi's *The Concubine* or that reflected in some of the popular Onitsha chapbooks which caution that 'women are very dangerous to men's lives' and that men die in many ways because of women and money.[27] Although he has been influenced by the Mammy Watta legend and the Fairmaid or Mermaid of Caribbean legend in his presentation of Simi,[28] he does present the complementary aspect of woman's personality.

Another positive element in Soyinka's presentation of woman is that he shows her capacity for independent action, noted particularly in the case of Iriyise, and for dominating men rather than being subservient to them. Two factors may have influenced Soyinka's presentation of women in this light. The first is Soyinka's natural admiration for the rebel. Iriyise and Segi are already rebels against societal norms which expect chastity before marriage, fidelity and obedience to one's husband afterwards, and a generally subservient role in a male-dominated society. Soyinka is also probably aware that such types of women already possess the daring temperament required to break taboos when necessary in order to achieve a desirable goal. This goal in the respective works is that of political change.

The other influence on Soyinka's characterization of the assertive woman may be his awareness of the singular freedom and independence of the typical Yoruba woman who is usually a trader. This is especially true of the women involved in long-distance trading. In addition, the economic independence that they often achieve serves to heighten their independence.[29] The resulting independence of spirit combined with an accompanying capacity for decisive action and plain speaking exude, for instance, from Iyaloja in *Death and the King's Horseman*; as the Iyalode of the market she performs a traditional ceremonial role which reflects the importance of the woman trader. She, along with the young women, spiritedly defies Amusa and the constables, speaks disparagingly to the Colonial District Officer Pilkings and bitterly denounces Elesin as the 'emptied bark that the world once saluted for a pith-laden being'. It is only when she fears that she may violate a taboo and endanger the psychic health of the tribe that she gives in to Elesin; and she undoubtedly emerges as stronger than all the other characters except Olunde.

Soyinka suggests that the asperity of temper displayed by the trader Amope, in *The Trials of Brother Jero*, is part of the survival kit of many Nigerian women:

> I think most of our, what you might call, petty trader character is very strong in a lot of our women. They are not quite as downtrodden as some people will have the world believe in these days of women's revolution. They know how to handle themselves.[30]

Another positive element in Soyinka's portrayal of women is his depiction of the ajé in *Madmen and Specialists*. It is their inclusion in the play which gives it a glimmer of hope. In the traditional Yoruba concept, the ajé or witches represent a fearful aspect of the hidden powers of women, and are among the malevolent forces who must be feared and propitiated.[31] As Iya Agba tells Iya Mate, 'Poison has its uses too. You can cure with poison if you use it right. Or kill'. The latter replies. 'You don't learn good things unless you learn evil'.[32] Soyinka's recognition of the inherent duality of experience, expressed here, enables him to present the positive/curative aspects of the witches as Earth Mothers instead of in their traditional role as agents of evil and destruction. Along with Si Bero, they are engaged in collecting curative herbs to augment Bero's store of medicinal drugs in the hope of aiding his post-war medical practice. They are symbols of hope and healing in the midst of a dehumanizing and somewhat bestial environment. Therefore, at the end of the play, the conflagration kindled by Iya Agba's pot of coals is supposed to be a purging by fire, the intervention of a cosmic force for redressing the balance between the forces of good and evil which co-exist in the universe. Both women, Iya Agba and Iya Mate, are representatives of this force; Iya Agba tells Bero, 'We move as the Earth moves, nothing more. We age as Earth ages'.[33] Woman here, in Si Bero and the Earth Mothers, functions as spiritual/moral leaven, though it is difficult to understand the material effect of their action on the socio-political reality.

However, even in presenting these 'revolutionary' images of woman, Soyinka remains a creature of his culture and his writing reflects the absorption of certain cultural attitudes towards women. For do we not also see this in the implied acceptance of a subservient role for the woman which allows Chume (*The Trials of Brother Jero*) finally to beat Amope and Egbo and Ofeyi to exploit their women sexually? His depiction of woman's maternal role in the sections 'of birth and death' and 'for women' in *Idanre and Other Poems* is a recognition of the traditional value attached to this particular woman's role. A concern with fecundity is illustrated by the association of sexual fulfilment with the future harvest of birth in 'Psalm' and 'Her Joy is Wild'.[34] Note the ecstatic **cry** of the fulfilled expectant mother in the latter poem:

> This is the last-born; give me
> A joyful womb to bind.

In 'To One, In Labour' Soyinka empathizes with the mother experiencing the lonely and excruciatingly painful contractions of labour:

> A Queen preparing . . .
> And the silent shrine of pain. In solitude
> Of catacombs the lethal arc contracts, my love –
> Of your secretions.[35]

Similarly, there is sympathetic presentations of the anguish of the bereaved mother of a stillborn child depicted in 'A Cry in the Night'.[36] The intensity of her grief is accentuated by her isolation as 'No stars caress her keening/The sky recedes from pain' and 'Night harshly folds her'.

There are glimpses of women in other roles such as the career woman, Dehinwa, (*The Interpreters*, pp. 66–7, 104–6) who has sufficient inner strength to resist the tribal prejudice and persistent interference of her mother in order to carry on her relationship with Sagoe. As a professional secretary she is self-possessed, unwilling to be goaded by Sagoe into a sexual relationship or the sharing of his absurd ideas on Voidancy. The impression she conveys is of a very business-like, competent and reliable woman capable of holding her own both within the business world and the social circle of the interpreters. Monica Faseyi and her mother-in-law, Mrs Faseyi, are also capable, coping women without the mysterious aura of Simi, Segi or Iriyise. However, these strong realistically presented women do not display much character development and their roles are peripheral. Soyinka needs to explore the personalities and possibilities of such women more comprehensively. With his known concern for the social values of literature in his role of social critic, his function might be heightened by the projection and exploration of more positive roles for women, roles which are being acted out by the Dehinwas and Monicas. This would not only complement the images of woman as political activist, siren, wife, mother, moral force and career woman but would simultaneously affect the verisimilitude of Soyinka's fictional world and perhaps further stimulate women into recognizing and acting out the new roles necessary for the 'land's transformation'.

NOTES

1. Wole Soyinka, *Collected Plays*, Vol. 1, London, Oxford University Press, 1973, pp. 101–4; *Camwood on the Leaves*, London, Methuen, 1973, pp. 1–9, 25–6.
2. Christine Purisch, 'Soyinka's Superwoman', Unpublished mimeographed MS presented at Ibadan Annual Literature Conference, 6–10 July, 1976, pp. 12–13.
3. Personal conversation with author at University of Ife, April 1977.
4. Samuel Johnson, *The History of the Yorubas*, Lagos, CMS Nigeria Bookshops, 1921, pp. 147–8.
5. Takiu Folami, 'Political Activities in Pre-Independence Nigeria', *Headlines* 51, June 1977, pp. 8–9.

6. Akin Mabogunje, 'The Market Woman', *Ibadan*, 11, February 1961, p. 15; Staff Society Reporter, 'Strong Woman of Nigeria Speaks Her Mind', *Africa*, May–June 1961, p. 15. See also *Africa Woman*, 4, April/May 1976, pp. 24–6.
7. Louis Gates, 'An Interview with Wole Soyinka', *Black World*, 4, August 1975, pp. 30–48; Biodun Jeyifo, 'Interview of Soyinka', *Transition*, 42, no. 8, 1973, pp. 62–4.
8. Sembène Ousmane, *God's Bits of Wood*, London, Heinemann, 1970, p. 266.
9. ibid., pp. 156–8, 185–202.
10. Wole Soyinka, *Season of Anomy*, London, Rex Collings, 1973, p. 219.
11. ibid., pp. 74–5.
12. ibid., pp. 45–9.
13. ibid., p. 20.
14. Ngugi wa Thiong'o, *Petals of Blood*, London, Heinemann, 1977, pp. 153–62, 200.
15. Soyinka, *Collected Plays*, Vol. 2, pp. 96–9.
16. ibid., pp. 97–8.
17. ibid., p. 98.
18. Soyinka, *Season of Anomy*, p. 8.
19. Wole Soyinka, *The Interpreters*, London, Heinemann, 1970, p. 125.
20. ibid., p. 54.
21. Soyinka, *Collected Plays*, Vol. 2, p. 104.
22. Soyinka, *Collected Plays*, Vol. 1, pp. 56–7.
23. D.H. Lawrence, *The Rainbow*, London, Penguin in association with William Heinemann, 1964 reprint, p. 463. See also pp. 322–480.
24. Soyinka, *Collected Plays*, Vol. 2, p 88.
25. Soyinka, *The Interpreters*, p. 123.
26. Soyinka, *Season of Anomy*, p. 82.
27. N.C. Njoku and Co, *Life, Money and Girls Turn Man Up and Down*, n.p., n.p., n.d; Gebo Brothers, *How to Start Life and End It Well*, 58 Venn Road, South Onitsha, n.p., n.d.
28. Chinua Achebe, *Morning Yet On Creation Day*, London, Heinemann, 1975, p. 92; Roy Heath, *A Man Come Home*, London, Longman, 1974, pp. 7, 89, 97–8, 109–18.
29. Niara Sudarkasa, *Where Women Work: A Study of Yoruba Women in the Marketplace and in the Home*, Museum of Anthropology, University of Michigan, no. 53, 1972, p. 66.
30. Karen L. Morrel, *In Person: Achebe, Awoonor and Soyinka at the University of Washington*, African Studies Program, Institute for Comparative and Foreign Area Studies, University of Washington, Seattle, 1975, p. 93.
31. Oyin Ogunba, *The Movement of Transition: A Study of the Plays of Wole Soyinka*, Ibadan, Ibadan University Press, 1975, p. 211; *Programme Booklet on Yoruba Oral Tradition*, Institute of African Studies, University of Ife, 12–19 January, 1974, p. 25.

32. Soyinka, *Collected Plays*, Vol. 2, pp. 225–6.
33. ibid., p. 259.
34. Wole Soyinka, *Idanre and Other Poems*, London, Eyre Methuen, 1974, pp. 34–5.
35. ibid., p. 38.
36. ibid., pp. 25–6.

Women and Resistance in Ngugi's *Devil on the Cross*

Jennifer Evans

While in the process of writing *Devil on the Cross* in detention, Ngugi explained in his prison diary the importance he attached to his heroine, Jacinta Wariinga:

> Because the women are the most oppressed and exploited section of the entire working class, I would create a picture of a strong determined woman with a will to resist and to struggle against the conditions of her present being. Had I not seen glimpses of this type in real life among the women of Kamīrīīthū Community Education and Cultural Centre? Isn't Kenyan history replete with this type of woman? Me Kitilili, Muraa wa Ngiti, Mary Mūthoni Nyanjirū? Mau Mau women cadres? Wariinga will be the fictional reflection of this resistance heroine of Kenyan history. Wariinga heroine of toil . . . there she walks . . .[1]

Ngugi evidently sees the image of Wariinga in an historical context, belonging to a feminine tradition of struggle and resistance found in both colonial and post-colonial Kenya. This concern with women is not new for Ngugi. All of his novels are sensitive to the burdens that Kenyan women have had to bear. Muthoni and Nyambura in *The River Between*, Njoroge's 'two mothers' in *Weep Not, Child*, Mumbi and Wangari in *A Grain of Wheat*, Wanja and Nyakinyua in *Petals of Blood*, are all in their own ways 'resistance heroines' and the strongest symbols of cultural identity, community and continuity that these novels have to offer.

Ngugi has portrayed modern Kenya as ruthless, immoral and avidly materialistic. The complexities and inequalities of this new society are especially well illustrated by the fate of Wanja in *Petals of Blood*. *Devil on the Cross* focuses even more emphatically on the particular dilemma of women in a rapidly changing society and their exploitation in terms of class and sex, using women's position as a measure of the ills of contemporary Kenya.

Devil on the Cross is the story of Jacinta Wariinga, ostensibly narrated by the 'Gicaandi Player' or 'Prophet of Justice' at the request of Jacinta's mother, 'so that each may pass judgement only when he knows the whole truth.'[2] In many respects the pattern of Waringa's life resembles that of Wanja in *Petals of Blood*. Both approximate to the exemplary tale of Kareendi, told by Waringa as the story of 'a girl like me . . . or . . . any other girl in Nairobi' (p. 17). Sexual exploitation and discrimination are dominant factors in Kareendi's life. She is given few opportunities to develop her potential and is constantly at the mercy of men for her livelihood. She is very often reduced to the cursed 'cunt' Wanja protests about in *Petals of Blood*.[3] For women like Kareendi there is no longer pride or joy in womanhood:

> To the Kareendis of modern Kenya, isn't each day exactly the same as all the others? For the day on which they are born is the very day on which every part of their body is buried except one – they are left with a single organ. So when will the Kareendis of modern Kenya wipe the tears from their faces? When will they ever discover laughter? (p. 26)

Even motherhood becomes a curse when the girl is young and unmarried and the man responsible will not admit it. While still at school, both Wanja and Waringa become pregnant by wealthy older men who abandon them. Wanja kills her baby. Waringa tries to kill herself, but is rescued. She is lucky enough to have a family who will take care of her child, and support her through secretarial college. She avoids Wanja's descent to the underworld of bars and prostitution, but must still face the disadvantages of her sex.

As a female office worker Waringa suffers sexual harassment and intimidation. She is not expected to be blatantly for sale like the barmaid, but she is expected to be available for the boss. Waringa comes to a fuller understanding of the nature of her dual exploitation as a worker and a woman in the course of the novel. Like Wanja, she realizes she must also choose her side: 'We who work as clerks, copy typists and secretaries, which side are we on? We who type and take dictation from *Boss* Kihara and his kind, whose side are we on in this dance? Are we on the side of the workers, or on the side of the rich? Who are we? Who are we?' (p. 206). Waringa sees that in exchange for a miserable salary, female office workers must sacrifice their 'arms', 'brains', 'humanity' and 'thighs' to serve their bosses (p. 206). Their exploitation is only a small part of the exploitation and expropriation which brings profits to the companies they work for. Waringa is

dismissed from the Champion Construction Company for refusing
to be Kihara's 'sugar girl'. Muturi is dismissed from the same company for organizing a strike against low wages. At the end of the
novel the same company is trying to take over the site of the garage
co-operative to build a tourist hotel, or, as the garage workers call
it, 'a factory for modern prostitution' (p. 223).

Wariinga is a 'resistance heroine' because she rises to the challenge which confronts her. The experience at the Devil's Feast
changes her from a spectator to a participant in the struggle. She
gains a positive image and self-esteem by fighting back, and by
refusing to accept the role ascribed to her. At the beginning of the
novel Wariinga's hatred of herself and her blackness shows in her
unbecoming appearance, spotted skin, singed hair, ill-fitting
clothes, and awkward movement. In three successive unjust blows,
men exert their power over her: her boss sacks her, her boyfriend
leaves her, and her landlord throws her out of her house. She is
defeated, confused and lacking in confidence. 'Insistent self-doubt
and crushing self-pity formed the burden that Wariinga was carrying that Saturday as she walked through the Nairobi streets . . .'
(p. 12). The final section of the novel (Chapters 10, 11 and 12)
commences two years after the Devil's Feast at Ilmorog, and is
principally concerned with the new dynamic Wariinga. She has
overcome daunting circumstances to deserve the title 'Wariinga,
heroine of toil.' Once her potential is not masked or crushed,
Wariinga becomes the beautiful woman she should be. By walking
on Muturi's 'paths of resistance' (p. 72) she has gained a pride in
her identity as a worker and as a black woman. She has achieved a
personal wholeness and will no longer tolerate being treated as a
'single organ'. Wariinga's movement and appearance now have a
unified perfection worthy of a true daughter of Mumbi:

> Today Wariinga strides along with energy and purpose, her dark eyes
> radiating the light of an inner courage, the courage and light of
> someone with firm aims in life – yes, the firmness and courage and
> faith of someone who has achieved something through self-reliance.
> What's the use of shuffling along timidly in one's own country?
> Wariinga, the black beauty! Wariinga of the mind and hands and body
> and heart, walking in rhythmic harmony on life's journey! Wariinga,
> the worker! (p. 218)

Wariinga works in a garage co-operative as a part-time car
mechanic, while completing a course in mechanical engineering at
the Polytechnic. She has dared to 'storm a man's citadel' (p. 220),

and, after some initial hostility and resistance, she has acquired respect and equality among fellow workers and students. She has also acquired physical and social confidence by learning karate and judo, and can adequately deal with any male intimidation. There is a touch of the invincibility of a comic-strip heroine about the new 'Wonder Woman' Wariinga, but Ngugi's portrayal of the karate-kicking car mechanic is obviously intended to carry a serious and important social meaning. Within the inequalities of the capitalist system, the novel as a whole lays heavy emphasis on the particular oppression of women in contemporary Kenya. Wariinga is above all important as a radical example of how a woman can resist being pushed, or tempted, into accepting subservient, degrading or decorative roles. Gaturia clearly explains Wariinga's social significance:

> We, the Kenyan youth, must be the light to light up new paths of progress for our country.
> You for instance, are a very good example of what I am trying to say. Your training in mechanical engineering, fitting and turning and moulding, is a very important step. It is a kind of signal to indicate to other girls their abilities and potential. (p. 244)

Wariinga learns to cope with urban life and modern technology. She is a positive model for a new generation of Kenyan women. A positive image of her traditional inheritance is represented by the figure of Wangari. Much like Nyakinyua in *Petals of Blood*, Wangari is the archetypal strong peasant woman, 'the tiller' (p. 44), the embodiment and symbol of Mother Kenya. Life on the land is extremely hard, but once she is dispossessed of her land Wangari finds her situation impossible. This woman, who has been a primary producer all her life, suddenly finds herself without useful employment. Her experiences in Nairobi highlight the problems of rapid social change and the particular difficulties faced by women in contemporary Kenyan society. Even an older woman like Wangari is insultingly treated as a sexual object. She explains that after she has told her troubles to one black shop manager, he laughs: 'He told me that the only job he could offer me was that of spreading my legs, that women with mature bodies were expert at that job' (p. 42). Wangari's innocent and honest attempt to find work eventually leads to arrest and jail. She is charged with vagrancy and intending to steal. A woman who has in the past been at the centre of her rural community, apparently has no right or place in the capital city of her country, and is dealt with as a trespasser. Wangari may be unfamiliar with the ways of modern urban life, but she does understand truth and justice. Women like Wangari and Nyakinyua, who are old enough to have participated in Mau Mau, possess the wisdom of the people's history. They have an acute political consciousness and are more secure in their cultural identity than younger women like Wariinga and Wanja. A hard-working woman of the soil, Wangari stands in extreme contrast to the idle bourgeois wives and mistresses who lead the kind of frivolous lives once reserved for white colonial women. Contestants at the Devil's Feast are required to declare their cars and their women in order to identify their wealth and status. Kihaahu wa Gatheeca proudly boasts in his testimony that his second wife has nothing to do: 'she has no job other than decking herself out in expensive clothes and jewellery for *cocktail parties*' (p. 109). Such personal indulgence and such a decorative passive role are completely alien to Wangari. She does not even have her ears pierced in the traditional fashion: ' "Because, ours was not a time for adorning our bodies with flowers and necklaces. Ours was a time for decorating ourselves with bullets in the fight for Kenya's freedom!" Wangari said with pride, because she knew that the deeds of her youth had changed Kenya's history' (p. 127). Wangari exemplifies the courage and spirit of the true Gikuyu woman, who has always participated in her people's struggles. It is in this image that the 'new' Wariinga is cast, and to this tradition that she belongs. Wangari is indeed a 'resistance heroine of Kenyan history' who can provide inspiration for the contemporary struggle, if she is acknowledged. Muturi, the politically conscious worker, recognizes her heroism and the fact that there are many women like her: 'Wangari, heroine of our country – all Wangaris, heroines of our land!' (p. 127). Gaturia, the intellectual, is also extremely impressed by Wangari's courageous behaviour when she brings the police to the cave, and they turn against her:

> Wangari raised her voice in song as they prodded at her and shoved her with clubs and batons and spat at her:
>> If ever you hear drip, drip, drip,
>> Don't think it's thundery rain.
>> No, it'll be the blood of us peasants
>> As we fight for our soil!
> And she was led out, still singing her defiance, her chained hands raised high above her head, the links gleaming like a necklace of courage. (p. 198)

Wangari does not need trinkets to decorate her body. Her beauty shines through her actions and transforms her chains. In his portrayal of Wangari, Ngugi acknowledges and pays tribute to the personal sacrifices and political contributions of peasant women. Within the task of historical retrieval and correction in which his novels are engaged this aspect is significant. Ngugi's fiction attempts to restore black men *and* black *women* to an active role in the making of their history.

While presenting the admirable qualities of the traditional rural woman, Ngugi does not seek to enshrine women in an irretrievable past. Coupled with his images of the traditional woman are images of 'new' women. Looking to the future, he points to paths of change and progress arising from his people's history. Warĩĩnga and Wanja are heiresses to a proud female tradition. Their portrayal constitutes an eloquent plea that women have a right to respect and equality in the modern world. Women must struggle to attain this for themselves, but Ngugi also draws attention to the prejudiced and oppressive behaviour of men as a major obstacle which must be consciously tackled. In *Devil on the Cross* Gaturia complains of the exploitation of Kenyan women by the tourist industry, but Warĩĩnga points out that the prejudices of Kenyan men are to blame, as well as the foreigners:

> Even you, the Kenyan men think that there is no job a woman can do other than cooking your food and massaging your bodies. . . . Why have people forgotten how Kenyan women used to make guns during the Mau Mau war against the British? Can't people recall the different tasks carried out by women in the villages once the men had been sent to detention camps? A song of praise begins at home. If you Kenyan men were not so scornful and oppressive, the foreigners you talk about so much would not be so contemptuous of us. (p. 245)

Ngugi portrays sexual confrontation between men and women as part of the destructive rivalry on which contemporary Kenyan capitalism thrives, and through which injustices and inequalities are perpetuated.

The ending of *Devil on the Cross* is optimistic in so far as it offers possibilities of new social orders in the future, but it is not conclusively 'happy'. Both Warĩĩnga and Gaturia go through enlightenment and liberation in the process of finding themselves and each other but, like the ill-fated lovers of Ngugi's earlier novels, they are to find that the larger social forces impinge on their personal relationship. The fact that there is no simple 'happy' ending reinforces the point, made in *Petals of Blood*, that 'La Luta Continua!' As Ngugi has said: 'The problem of men and women cannot be satisfactorily solved under the present system. Sexual relations are the reflection of an unequal economic system.'[4] Wariinga refuses to settle down to marriage with Gaturia, because she discovers that her prospective father-in-law is her seducer, 'the Rich Old Man from Ngorika'. When Wangari delivers her condemnation of the thieves at the Devil's Feast 'her voice carried the power and authority of a people's judge' (p. 197). Wariinga also speaks with the voice of 'a people's judge' when she condemns the Rich Old Man to die (p. 253). Wariinga's execution of her oppressor, like Wanja's execution of Kimeria in *Petals of Blood*, is more than personal revenge. It carries the force of communal retribution and justice.

Both Wariinga and Wanja rise above the tale of Kareendi because they do not finally accept defeat and humiliation. Having come to the realization that there are more than the 'two worlds' of 'the eater' and 'the eaten', Wariinga commits herself to the 'third world': 'the world of the revolutionary overthrow of the system of eating and being eaten' (p. 188).

Ngugi has tailored the content, form and style of *Devil on the Cross* for his intended Gikuyu-speaking worker and peasant audience. His only concession to his foreign readers is to have made an English translation. Properly the work should be read aloud and communally in its original Gikuyu. An individual private reading of the English version can obviously not do justice to a work whose principal significance lies in its use of the Gikuyu language. But, in a novel which is so intimately concerned with Ngugi's individual and communal identity, it is also significant that images of women are such a prominent feature. Wariinga the female protagonist of *Devil on the Cross*, is the successor to a line of heroines who have become increasingly central to the structure and meaning of Ngugi's novels.

The significant interplay of female images in Ngugi's life and literature is evident in *Detained*. He begins the first chapter of his prison diary with a direct reference to his fictional Gikuyu heroine: '*Wariinga ngatha ya wira* . . . Wariinga heroine of toil . . . there she walks haughtily carrying her freedom in her hands . . .' (p. 3) The second section of this chapter begins with Ngugi's contemplation of a photograph of his daughter Njooki, born to his wife Nyambura five months after his arrest, and the various names she has been given: 'Njooki, meaning she who comes back from the dead; or Aiyerubo, meaning she who defies heaven and hell; or

Wamũingĩ, meaning she who belongs to the people.' (p. 12)
Warĩĩnga and Njooki are both sources of inspiration and courage,
of sanity and optimism, in the cruel and uncertain world of detention. In the third and concluding section of Chapter 1, Ngugi
coalesces the images of Njooki and Warĩĩnga. As symbolic links
with history and community, with the world beyond the prison
walls, they give strength and meaning to Ngugi's resistance:

> Njooki, a picture sent through the post; and Warĩĩnga, a picture created
> on rationed toilet paper, have been more than a thousand trumpets
> silently breaking through the fortified walls of Kamĩtĩ Maximum Secu-
> rity Prison to assure me that I am not alone; Warĩĩnga by constantly
> making me conscious of my connection with history, and Njooki, by
> constantly making me aware that I am now in prison because of
> Kamĩrĩĩthũ and its people.
>
> But Warĩĩnga and Njooki also keep on reminding me that my deten-
> tion is not a personal affair. It's part of the wider history of attempts to
> bring up the Kenyan people in a reactionary culture of silence and fear,
> and of the Kenyan people's fierce struggle against them to create a
> people's revolutionary culture of outspoken courage and patriotic
> heroism. (pp. 27–8)

Considering the symbolic strength of the image of the pregnant
woman and the possibilities for the future that she carries, which
are finally represented by Mumbi in *A Grain of Wheat* and by
Wanja in *Petals of Blood*, the dynamic relationship between
Ngugi's life and his art is well illustrated by the fact that in detention he should himself be sustained by the images of a woman and a
child. In the heroine of *Devil on the Cross* and his own daughter, he
finds compelling symbolic value: 'Warĩĩnga . . . Njooki . . . my symbols of hope and defiance.' (p. 167) In the actual creation of human
life through a woman, and the literary creation of the figure of a
woman, Ngugi sees the essence of his own struggle and the communal struggle of the people of Kenya.

NOTES

1. Ngugi wa Thiong'o, *Detained. A Writer's Prison Diary*, London,
   Heinemann, 1981, p. 10. All subsequent references are to this edition
   and appear in the text.

2. Ngugi wa Thiong'o, *Devil on the Cross*, trans. from the Gikuyu by the author, London, Heinemann, 1982, p. 7. All subsequent references are to this edition and appear in the text.
3. Ngugi wa Thiong'o, *Petals of Blood*, London, Heinemann, 1977, p. 293.
4. Anita Shreve. '*Petals of Blood*, an interview with Ngugi', *Viva*, Nairobi, 3, no. 6, 1977, p. 35.

The House of Slavery

Adewale Maja-Pearce

One of the most persistent themes in modern African literature is that of the relationship between the European woman and the African man. How successfully the writers have handled this theme will tell us a lot about their response to their recent history, the rape of their continent by the European powers over the last four centuries. This is inescapable. All Africans have ambivalent attitudes towards Europeans precisely because of this imbalance in their respective histories. The terms on which the African meets the European is determined by the extent to which he has come to terms with this imbalance. The more intimate the relationship the more revealing the state of mind; and no relationship is more intimate than that which is possible between a man and a woman. This means that the European woman, the white woman, is invested with a symbolic significance: in her person she is made to bear the burden of her people.

Dele, the hero of Kole Omotoso's *The Edifice*, claims to find white women loathsome:

> Imagine mother thinking I could ever descend to marry a white girl! What a thought!. . . How could a white woman be beautiful? There was the one I had seen at a swimming pool at home. She looked like two dry bamboo poles, a crucifix in a bikini. All shrivelled up. Finished. After only two confinements . . . Put her by the side of the black beautiful. The older a black woman gets the more beautiful she becomes.[1]

But this does not stop him sleeping with them. Not that it is his fault, since they are cheap; as a friend explains:

> To most of them sex doesn't mean a thing. All the sacredness you people attach to it doesn't exist as far as they're concerned. So don't be surprised if after a girl has spent the night with you, she sees you later in the day and wouldn't say 'Hello'. It is just their way of life. (p. 87)

And yet, just before he is due to return home, he meets Daisy, an Englishwoman and fellow-student, and proposes marriage to her.

Has he, then, been regenerated by love? Here he is at the marriage ceremony:

> All through that marriage service I kept on remembering a funeral service I'd attended years ago. It was cold in the church. Very cold. There were a few of my friends . . . Those who came looked as if they were at a funeral ceremony. My funeral. (p. 92)

Hardly complimentary to his bride, but never mind. They go to Nigeria, where Daisy takes up the narrative. This is damaging to the structure of the novel, but it has a purpose.

Almost as soon as they arrive Dele starts behaving atrociously. He comes and goes as he pleases, stays out all night, and then shouts at her when she begs him to tell her how she is to behave:

> Please, Dele . . . how did your grandfather's wives plead with him? Did they call him their lord, the commander of all their wishes? (p. 100)

She grovels. This is the signal for him to begin destroying her. He starts by beating her up:

> He pushed me down. I banged against the french window. He hit out wildly and his punch caught me on the left side of my head. I reeled and fell down. He began to kick me, mechanically, not caring where. I remember his foot making contact from one moment to another. (p. 103)

It is a wonder he does not kill her, but then he has more in store for her:

> One night I heard voices in his bedroom. There was a thin black girl in bed with him. It was a shock to me. How could he do it? Did he not love me? Was I not carrying his child? . . . When I complained to him he said I should not worry him. (p. 112)

At this point, one would have thought, even the most docile of women would have snapped; not so Daisy. Her humiliation must be complete, which is why she is made to recount it herself. She eventually talks herself into accepting the situation:

> I accepted the part of Dele having girl-friends and even of his bringing them to the same bed in which our unborn baby had been conceived. I was still his wife. (p. 112)

Her destruction is sealed with the ritual murder of her son at the hands of her mother-in-law, the same woman who had warned Dele not to return home with a white wife:

> . . . shortly after his fourth birthday he was taken to the provinces to visit his grandparents. I did not want him to go, but by this time I had lost any influence I ever had with my husband. Dele junior went, but he never came back. I was told later on that he'd fallen down a well. I never knew whether or not his body was fished out of the well and buried. I couldn't ask. But I knew in my innermost heart that my child had been murdered. My mother-in-law did not like the child. (p. 118)

Is the author suggesting that Nigerians are in the habit of murdering their own children? More to the point, are we to believe that this is a mother talking? Or has she been created purely in order to be destroyed? There is nothing real about her. It is as if vengeance is being exacted upon her for the four centuries of European history in Africa; and to be destroyed Daisy must first be possessed, which is why Dele must marry her despite his protestations that he hates white women. And he does hate them. But it is not a simple hatred. He also loves them with that twisted love of the victim who has believed everything his oppressor has told him about himself. His hatred is a complex hatred, in other words, and complex, at last, because it is a self-hatred. He despises himself, he believes himself to be inferior, and so he must prove to himself and to the world that this is not so; and how more completely can he prove it than by having one of them say to him, as Daisy does after he has deliberately and wilfully humiliated her: 'I'm half-crazy all for the love of you'? (p. 102). If she can still say this then perhaps he really is her equal.

Mbella Sonne Dipoko's *A Few Nights and Days* also has a student as its central character, though this time the action takes place in France. Doumbe is involved with a nineteen-year-old fellow-student, Thérèse. His attitude towards her is made clear from the start: 'Her feelings for me were a mixture of love and gratefulness; mine were tinged with a profound sense of responsibility'; 'Thérèse was lovingly naive . . . She was younger in mind than her nineteen years. I didn't like that at all. It aroused pity in me . . .'[2] he remarks, thereby establishing at once, in case we were in any doubt, his superiority over her. But he shows what he really thinks of her by carrying on a secret affair with her best friend, Bibi, a slightly older and more experienced woman. He attempts to deny that contempt for Thérèse is the real reason for his action by claiming that it is because:

. . . I was going to write. I had to live, and the pleasure which women gave, their life, was the very depth of existence. I liked women. I shall write and immortalize their names . . . those who had been before . . . and those who will come after. (p. 65)

For sheer cynicism this would be hard to equal. He has very little trouble seducing Bibi. She is the woman as whore who shows almost no remorse in betraying her friendship, and as if that weren't complicated enough she is also supposed to be having an affair with Laurent, a white man and latent homosexual. The white man as homosexual is an important sub-theme. We find it in Omotoso's novel in the guise of an English teacher (the only white man in the entire novel) who tries to seduce Dele while the latter is still a schoolboy. This is because the destruction of the white woman is achieved largely through sex, and so the white man, who cannot be allowed to be a threat, must be rendered impotent. All the white men in Dipoko's novel are sexually dubious and incapable of satisfying their women. Apart from Laurent there is Doumbe's landlady's son, whom we never actually meet:

Madame Bistrott told me that François didn't want to get married. She said it was a matter of principle. He didn't want women. She used to say it was funny, wasn't it, that François didn't want women and yet he was such a decent boy; then, she would add, 'he's fifty, you know!' (p. 90)

And then there's Thérèse's father, Monsieur Vaele:

Thérèse's father, Bibi told me, was very sensitive. I said we all were, so what? She said he was too much so. He always suspected his wife and daughter were making fun of him. And since he wouldn't have it, he insisted on his wife behaving in a way that would convince him that she respected him. This had led to a kind of tyranny. Thérèse's mother was its main victim. (p. 39)

The corollary of this view of the white man is that only the black man is capable of satisfying white women, and that the black man's weight in the world is to be measured exclusively in terms of his sexual performance.

Without warning Doumbe suddenly proposes marriage to Thérèse:

There was something true and human about Thérèse that deepened my feelings for her; sometimes I thought if I didn't marry her I'd never marry another woman . . . (p. 113)

But Monsieur Vaele is opposed to the marriage, not, he assures Doumbe, because he's black, but because he cannot bear the thought of his only child going to live so far away from him. Doumbe, playing the traditional African, explains that however much he might love her he will never marry her without Monsieur Vaele's permission because:

> Marriage is not between two persons. It is between two families. That is how it is in Africa. Marriage brings two families together, not just two persons. (p. 108)

Even more nobly, he agrees to keep this a secret from Thérèse, since Monsieur Vaele is terrified of his daughter's wrath:

> 'Thérèse mustn't know of my decision. If she does she'd be furious with me. And her anger can be terrible.' (p. 109)

And this, mind you, of an ineffectual and 'lovingly naive' nineteen-year-old. They decide that Doumbe will string her along for a month or so and then quietly disappear. The cruelty of this escapes the pair of them altogether. Conveniently enough Doumbe has only just received a letter from his father recalling him home, one of those coincidences which finally renders the novel implausible. He keeps up the pretence superbly until, a week before he is due to leave, the truth comes out while they are all having dinner together. Thérèse is thunderstruck, as well she might be. Doumbe immediately absolves himself from responsibility by declaring himself willing to marry her at once if her father will give his permission. He refuses. That night she commits suicide. It is Bibi who gives him the news the following day. Thérèse's destruction, all for the love of him, is that much sweeter for having been accomplished by her own hand. Doumbe wins on all fronts. As a final twist Bibi announces that she is pregnant by him (how could it be by Laurent?), but that she doesn't bear him any ill-will:

> It won't be easy for me . . . especially as this will be my second child. But I'm not angry with you. Truly I'm not. (p. 184)

She is made to play the whore to the end. Her destruction is perhaps the more invidious because she is made to discard herself even before Doumbe can do so: she knows that she's worthless, which is even better than having to be told it.

Yulisa Amadu Maddy's *No Past, No Present, No Future* is

another novel which deals with this theme, but in a slightly more subtle way than either *The Edifice* or *A Few Nights and Days*. Santigie, one of three Africans studying in England, is used as the foil against which the actions of the other two characters are to be measured. When Joe tells him:

> I am not ashamed to admit that by going to bed with white women I regard them purely as victims. . . . Let me tell you that the only way I can get my own back for the victimization, degradation, and defeat I have suffered, is to do this. It is my only weapon. . . .
> Here in this room, I tell my women victims that they are paying colonial debts. I make them pay debts of conscience with their white skins.[3]

he retorts by saying:

> But aren't you becoming perverted yourself? Aren't you succumbing to the same vices which you are protesting about? (p. 164)

But – and this is surely the point, Joe is a homosexual, incapable of forming any kind of relationship with a woman. And it is the third character, Ade, who is then used to wreak vengeance on the white woman. We learn about Ade at the outset:

> he excelled with women. . . . For him, women were to be relished sexually. That's what they were there for. (p. 46)

This is supposed to be the excuse for his subsequent behaviour.

In a pub in Hampstead he meets Bodil, a beautiful Danish woman who quickly falls in love with him. When she becomes pregnant he decides to marry her, for which purpose they travel to Denmark so that her parents can be present at the wedding. No sooner do they arrive than he starts an affair with her best friend, Lona. The parallels between Lona and Bibi are remarkable. They are both Scandinavian, for instance, and therefore 'cheap': both the authors have fallen for the stereotype of the Scandinavian woman as sexually available at the same time as they compound the stereotype of the African male as sexually promiscuous. Unlike Bibi, however, Lona is quickly put in her place. After an evening with her Ade muses to himself:

> Lona, you are a drunk . . . a pathetic drunk. Overbearing, a man-devouring monster. What would I do with you? How could I introduce you to my friends? You would drink me under the table . . . you drunken nurse. (p. 143)

But what does that make him? And it is Lona who is used as the instrument to destroy Bodil, just as Monsieur Vaele was used to destroy Thérèse. Lona convinces herself that it is really she whom Ade loves, and informs Bodil of this by letter. She is also pregnant by him. Bodil at least has more spunk than either Daisy or Thérèse; she orders Ade to leave, though he does not exactly plead with her for forgiveness. But she has been spoiled forever:

> I couldn't take another boy-friend. I couldn't. Even if I wasn't pregnant, I love him so much. If only he knew. Oh God! (p. 142)

Why these women should be so consistently betrayed by their best friends is a mystery, unless they are being unconsciously used to deflect criticism from the men: I might behave in such-and -such a way, the men seem to be saying, but look at what they do to one another.

The best that can be said for Peter Abrahams' *A Wreath for Udomo* is that he uses the best-friend-as-betrayer with a little more sophistication. Udomo, the hero, meets and falls in love with an Englishwoman, Lois, while still a student. He moves in with her and her flatmate, Jo, who is also her best friend. One day while Lois is at work, Jo seduces Udomo, but not until we are presented with a fairly sympathetic portrait of her which accounts, in some part, for what she does: She lacks confidence as a result of an unhappy childhood. This is popular psychology at its most hackneyed, but it will do. Yet when all is said and done she is still a whore, and therefore to be despised:

> She'd do anything if only he didn't make her feel so filthy. Made her feel she was dirt . . . And yet she loved him. Filthy dirt. An easy man to love. Some children have mothers. I never had one. If I had a mother now I would kneel in front of her and put my head on her lap and tell her all my troubles . . . I only had a father who married another woman and made me want to leave home as soon as I could. A filthy dirty little tart, his eyes say. Oh God! Is it wrong to want to be loved?[4]

Inevitably she becomes pregnant. Udomo arranges for a friend of his, a medical student, to give her an abortion. Because of complications the treatment takes longer than anticipated and Lois returns home while it is still going on.

What is striking about all the women in these novels is their immaturity. None of them can be considered fully adult. This is part and parcel of the writers' own immature handling of the theme, and their inability, or unwillingness, to confront the real problem squarely: namely, that of their relation to their history, and to the people they hold responsible for it.

Tayeb Salih's women are at least adults, and his novel is the better for it. Not that their subsequent destruction is any less complete. *Season of Migration to the North* recounts the story, largely in his own words, of Mustafa Sa'eed, now middle-aged, as he makes his way from a small and 'backward' North African village first to Cairo and then to University in the England of the 1920s. He is a brilliant student. He absorbs with ease the intellectual tradition of his conquerors and uses it to 'better' himself. While in England he becomes obsessed with an Englishwoman, Jean Morris, whom he pursues relentlessly:

> . . . against my will, I fell in love with her and I was no longer able to control the course of events. When I avoided her she would entice me to her, and when I ran after her she fled from me.[5]

In the end she agrees to marry him, but even then she remains unattainable:

> For two months she wouldn't let me near her; every night she would say, 'I'm tired' or 'I'm unwell.' (p. 158)

Whenever they go out together she flirts outrageously and creates scenes in order to goad him:

> Once in a pub she suddenly shouted, 'That son of a bitch is making passes at me.' I sprang at the man and we seized each other by the throat. People collected round us and suddenly behind me I heard guffawing with laughter. One of the men who had come to separate us said to me, 'I'm sorry to have to tell you, if this woman's your wife, you've married a whore.' (p. 161)

Returning home one cold February evening he finds her stretched out naked on the bed, her thighs spread open:

> Though her lips were formed into a full smile, there was something like sadness on her face; it was as though she was in a state of great readiness both to give and to take. (p. 163)

She denies that anyone has been with her. He takes a knife from its sheath and sits on the edge of the bed:

Then she took hold of the dagger and kissed it fervently. Suddenly she closed her eyes and stretched out in the bed, raising her middle slightly, opening her thighs wider. 'Please my sweet,' she said, moaning: 'Come – I'm ready now.' When I did not answer her appeal she gave a more agonizing moan. She waited. She wept. Her voice was so faint it could hardly be heard. 'Please, darling.'

'Here are my ships, my darling, sailing towards the shores of destruction.' I leant over and kissed her. I put the blade-edge between her breasts and she twined her legs round my back. Slowly I pressed down. Slowly. She opened her eyes. What ecstasy there was in those eyes! She seemed more beautiful than anything in the whole world. 'Darling,' she said painfully, 'I thought you would never do this. I almost gave up hope of you.' I pressed down the dagger with my chest until it had all disappeared between her breasts. I could feel the hot blood gushing from her chest. I began crushing my chest against her as she called out imploringly: 'Come with me. Don't let me go alone.' (pp. 164–5)[6]

So she invites her own destruction. And the incident convinces partly because she has already been presented as a strange and elusive person:

She used to lie about the most extraordinary things and would return home with amazing and incredible stories about incidents that had happened to her and people she'd met. (p. 155)

Or again:

Once, taking hold of myself, I kept away from her for two weeks . . . Nevertheless, she found her way to my house and surprised me late one Saturday night when Ann Hammond was with me. She heaped filthy curses on Ann Hammond, and when I tried to drive her away with blows she was not deterred. Ann Hammond left in tears, while she stayed on, standing in front of me like some demon, a challenging defiance in her eyes that stirred remote longings in my heart. Without our exchanging a word, she stripped off her clothes and stood naked before me. (p. 156)

Salih is clearly probing greater depths than any of the other novelists. He is exploiting, in a world still dominated by male values, the old and universal myth of the woman as both goddess and whore who must be simultaneously worshipped and destroyed. But it is significant that he uses the European and not the African woman as the symbol. That he doesn't succumb to simple-minded hate is demonstrated by the insight he shows into the real meaning of the European conquest of Africa; in Mustafa Sa'eed's words:

The white man, merely because he has ruled us for a period of our history, will for a long time continue to have for us that feeling of contempt the strong have for the weak . . . But their . . . coming was not a tragedy as we imagine, nor yet a blessing as they imagine. It was a melodramatic act which the passage of time will change into a mighty myth. (p. 60)

This seems to me absolutely correct, an altogether more objective view of the real meaning of the African past.

Ayi Kwei Armah's *Why Are We So Blest?* is probably the most objectionable of all the African novels which deal with this theme. Here is the narrator, Solo, examining his condition:

What is ordained for us I have not escaped – the fate of the *évolué*, the turning of the assimilated African, not into something creating its own life, but into an eater of crumbs in the house of slavery.[7]

This is because he is at the mercy of his hate. Solo hates white women with a passion. Entering a night-club one evening he catches sight of a black man and a white woman together. The sight fills him with revulsion:

Before this night the sight of white women with black men turned me to thoughts of love. Now I don't even think of slave and mistresses. I see in each happy black man carrion – fastened onto by a beast of prey. (p. 269)

The novel tells the story of Modin, yet another young African studying abroad, this time in America, who becomes disillusioned with academic life and decides to return to Africa to fight in a colonial war. While in America he meets Aimée, a white woman and fellow-student. From the start she is portrayed as sexually perverted. She can only climax by fantasizing that Modin is her houseboy and that her husband, a white settler gone to the African bush to hunt down revolutionaries, is expected home any minute. Modin discovers her fantasy when she inadvertently calls out his fictitious name at the moment of climax:

'The rebellion, my period. My husband is coming home. He's a settler. I don't know when. It's dangerous. You're the boy.'
And Mwangi is my name.
'Yes, yes, yes, yes, dooon't stop! Yes!' (p. 199)

So Modin is reduced to a 'boy', the black buck with whom Aimée satisfies her perverted sexuality. But this, apparently, doesn't bother him because when he leaves for Africa, a few weeks later, he takes her with him.

They go first to a neighbouring African country and hang around the headquarters-in-exile of the liberation movement, hoping to be smuggled into the warring country. But the two representatives at the headquarters have no intention of helping them. For one thing they, too, share the general disgust for white women; as one of them puts it:

> . . . an African in love with a European is a pure slave. Not a man accidentally enslaved. A pure slave, with the heart of a slave, with the spirit of a slave. (p. 255)

So in the end they take it upon themselves to hitch-hike across the desert and enter under their own steam. In the desert they are set upon by four white men who strip Modin and tie him to the back of their jeep, arms spread-eagled, feet off the ground, in the manner of a crucifixion. They also strip Aimée and brush her against him so that he has an erection. Then they rape her, one by one. Afterwards two of the men tie a length of thin wire around the end of Modin's penis and jerk it tight so that it cuts through the flesh and leaves the end dangling by a piece of skin. All this is described in great detail by Aimée in her journal. Then:

> Modin started bleeding. The blood curved out in a little stream that jerked outward about every second. I reached him and without thinking of what I was doing I kissed him. His blood filled my mouth. I swallowed it. I wanted him to speak to me. He had groaned a little when I took him and kissed him, but he said nothing.
> I asked him 'Do you love me?' (p. 288)

This scene is shocking and disgusting, but not in the way it is intended to be. We aren't shocked by Aimée's behaviour because Aimée is no more real than Daisy or Thérèse or Bodil. The writer has gone too far. This is pure fantasy, and it arouses in the reader the suspicion that a symbolic self-castration is at work here.

The novel's originality lies only in the fact that the hero is himself overtly destroyed, along with the woman; but the hatred of the white woman, symbol of his oppression, is no less vicious. What all these novels demonstrate is the enormous complexity of the African's response to the white world. For all the hatred of the white woman, the fact remains that she cannot be left alone. There is something sinister and even pathological in the relentlessness of their pursuit of her, as though their lives depended on getting her into their beds to show off their virility. Hence, of course, the staggering number of pregnancies.

What does all this mean then? Simply, that Africans have not yet liberated themselves from their past, if the literature is anything to go by. It means that they are still at the mercy of their history, and as long as this is so their history will remain a tyranny to them. And, after all, such hatred is futile and childish. It gets us nowhere. It produces a limited and negative view of the world and of our place in it. It keeps us dependent on others' possibly distorted perception of us, particularly the demeaning and prurient image of the black man as stud. This is an intolerable position to be in. After four centuries of dependence the time has surely come for us to begin to assert ourselves.

NOTES

1. Kole Omotoso: *The Edifice*, London, Heinemann, 1971, p. 49. All subsequent references are to this edition and appear in the text.
2. Mbella Sonne Dipoko, *A Few Nights and Days*, London, Heinemann, 1977, first published 1970, pp. 27–8. All subsequent references are to this edition and appear in the text.
3. Yulisa Amadu Maddy, *No Past, No Present, No Future*, London, Heinemann, 1977, first published 1973, pp. 163–4. All subsequent references are to this edition and appear in the text.
4. Peter Abrahams, *A Wreath for Udomo*, London, Faber, 1956, pp. 102–3.
5. Tayeb Salih, *Season of Migration to the North*, London, Quartet Books, 1980, first published London, Heinemann, 1969, p. 156. All subsequent references are to this edition and appear in the text.
6. It is interesting that Tayeh Salih is the only one of these writers who is a Muslim. One is reminded of the Muslim practice of infibulation when reading this passage, which also uses a dagger or knife to mutilate women.
7. Ayi Kwei Armah, *Why Are We So Blest?* London, Heinemann, 1974, first published New York, Doubleday, 1972, p. 84. All subsequent references are to this edition and appear in the text.

The Afro-American– West African Marriage Question: Its Literary and Historical Contexts

Brenda F. Berrian

Marriages and the relationships between husbands and wives represent common subjects in virtually every African literary genre. Rarely, however, do critics of African literature subject these phenomena to close critical analyses. Further, another type of marriage between Afro-Americans and West Africans, though clearly reflected in both Afro-American and English-speaking African literature, is hardly talked about. This paper intends to correct this oversight.

Intercultural marriages, particularly between Afro-Americans and West African men, are growing at an increasing rate. Motivations for these marriages reside in a combination of conscious and unconscious factors which will be discussed during the course of the essay. When one talks about intercultural marriages between Afro-Americans and West Africans one expects that they will be interpreted within the context of time and place. Most of these marriages are the culmination of contemporary university romances in American, European and African settings.

Romance between an Afro-American and a West African serves as a secondary theme in Lorraine Hansberry's play, *A Raisin in the Sun* (1959) and as a primary theme in Ama Ata Aidoo's play, *The Dilemma of a Ghost* (1965). *A Raisin in the Sun* is a three-act play which opened on Broadway on 11 March 1959, and captured the Drama Circle Critics Award as the best play that year. Its Afro-American author, the now deceased Lorraine Hansberry, was only 29 years old at the time of the performance. *The Dilemma of a Ghost*, a five-act play which was presented by the Students'

Theatre, at the University of Ghana, Legon on the 12, 13 and 14 March 1964 was written by a 20-year old Ghanaian woman. Thus, these themes were highlighted in the works of youthful writers.

As a secondary theme, possible marriage between a Nigerian male student and an Afro-American woman appears in the incidental passages in *A Raisin in the Sun*, the primary theme of which is the determination of a lower-middle class Afro-American family to better their standing in American society by moving from the slums to the suburbs. More broadly speaking, the play is about choices, about a son's struggle to find his manhood, and about the reaffirmation of black identity. The theme of an intercultural marriage can be viewed as a testimony of self-affirmation, new freedoms and a positive step towards black identity.

Joseph Asagai, the Nigerian male student in *A Raisin in the Sun*, brings a set of new ideas and values to the theme of an Afro-American who is searching for a new lease of life and a quick, easy way to beat the system. Asagai is presented as a self-assured, well-travelled and well-spoken individual who is Beneatha Younger's pathway to a completed search for her identity. Through his marriage proposal to Beneatha he offers a promise of life in a soon-to-be independent Nigeria as opposed to life in Chicago as a wife to a bourgeois Afro-American with all the dullness and pretentiousness that the latter entails.

Beneatha is portrayed as a 20-year old woman who is restless, unsettled, bored, studying to be a doctor and in search of something new, different, and alien to her environment. Asagai and his stories about Nigeria bring a breath of fresh air to an otherwise stifling, and almost intolerable situation. Beneatha's relationship with Asagai makes her aware of the desire of Afro-Americans to merge into the dominant American society. This is shown in Beneatha's conversation with her sister-in-law and her Afro-American boyfriend, George:

RUTH:　Why must you and your brother make an argument out of everything people say?

BENEATHA:　Because I hate assimilationist Negroes!

RUTH:　Will somebody tell me what assimila-who-means!

GEORGE:　Oh, it's just a college girl's way of calling people Uncle Toms – but that isn't what it means at all.

RUTH:　Well, what does it mean?

BENEATHA:　(*Cutting George off and staring at him as she replies to Ruth*): It means someone who is willing to give up his own culture and submerge himself completely in the dominant, and in this case, oppressive culture![1]

This conversation and an earlier one that takes place when Mama Younger asks Beneatha 'Why should I know about Africa?' illustrates the limited knowledge that most Afro-Americans have of Africa. Consequently, the popular *A Raisin in the Sun* helped to usher in a new awareness of Africa which would develop and mature among Afro-Americans from the late 1950s to the present. Some Afro-Americans represented by Mama and George who had been bombarded with false Tarzan-inspired images will not be able to make a positive identification with Africa.

Kwame Nkrumah's open invitation to Afro-Americans to come to Ghana when that country became independent in 1957, and the arrival of African representatives to the United Nations, encouraged Afro-Americans to replace their feelings of indifference, rejection, and shame for Africa with those of acceptance, pride, and appreciation. Africa became visible, an important news item, and many Afro-Americans like Hansberry's Beneatha seized the opportunity to identify in a positive way with the African continent. Eventual marriages between Africans and Afro-Americans was a most natural next step. Asagai's proposal of marriage to Beneatha comes as a surprise neither to the readers nor to the audience of the Hansberry play.

At the opposite pole Asagai's rival, George Murchison, represents 'money', for he is from a well-established Afro-American middle-class family. For Beneatha's family, George represents good husband material, for money means security and stability – something that the Youngers themselves want. They encourage Beneatha to consider George; however, he does not fit into Beneatha's current plans to find her African heritage. George, in turn, cannot understand her curiosity and even rejects being called 'Black Brother' by Beneatha's brother, Walter Younger. He considers Beneatha's African robe 'eccentric' and rejects the lecture on the 'Great West African Heritage'. George plainly tells Beneatha that Africa may reflect her heritage, but not his, and 'is nothing but a bunch of raggedy-assed spirituals and some grass huts.' (p. 68)

On another level, George is not sensitive enough to notice that Beneatha's intellectual as well as physical needs have to be stroked. Asagai, on the other hand, appeals to Beneatha's intellectual and psychological needs. Beneatha is at the stage where she wants to feel at ease and be encouraged to philosophize and express her opinions.

In Act III of *A Raisin in the Sun*, Asagai tries to comfort Beneatha when she reveals her unhappiness because her brother, Walter, has misused the money set aside for her college education. She predicts that things will be just the same in Africa when the black man is in power. Asagai replies that at least it will be the black man's fate, determined by himself and the substance of truth, rather than by only Western standards of civilization or as Julian Mayfield states it, by 'diehard integrationists'.[2] This philosophy and Asagai's proposal leave Beneatha confused and shaken, which is an attestation of Lorraine Hansberry's own confused notions of the role of intercultural marriages.[3]

While Lorraine Hansberry leaves her reader/audience wondering what will be Beneatha's answer to Asagai's proposal, the Ghanaian author, Ama Ata Aidoo, produces a reply in her play, *The Dilemma of a Ghost*. The plot of *The Dilemma of a Ghost* is essentially about a troubled marriage between a Ghanaian groom, Ato Yawson, and his Afro-American bride Eulalie Rush. The two meet at college, marry in the United States, and return to Ghana without first warning Ato's family. The play deals with the following issues: (1) Ghanaian ideas about the status of women; (2) the wife's relationship to her husband's family; (3) patterns of contradictions and ambivalences; (4) opposing cultures and life styles. Eulalie, like Beneatha, dreams of belonging to a heroic ancestral land, but she is not automatically accepted or welcomed by her in-laws who know that she has no family in Harlem. Eulalie is seen by her in-laws as an outsider and a descendant of slaves who therefore belongs to no distinct ethnic African group.

Ato is weaker than Eulalie for he finds it impossible to reconcile or synthesize two cultures – his traditional past and the contemporary Western present. He should be the intermediary between Eulalie and his family and the equalizer of two opposing cultures and life styles; for the success of an intercultural marriage, like any other kind, depends on the backgrounds and maturity of the two people involved. For the Yawson marriage to survive, the two principals must combine those customs or mores that will suit them in a Ghanaian setting. They must also work towards an understanding between themselves and Ato's family. The Ato characters are, however, unable to achieve this. Instead, a lack of understanding and recognition of different cultural mores and value systems result from the couple's preconceived interpretations of marriage. Eulalie, a product of urban Harlem, has been raised to behave as if her marriage is a private matter without external familial constraints. This attitude is in stark contrast to Ato's customs and traditions, which govern a conflict in a marriage. Traditionally, his family plays an important role in instructing a young married couple. Eulalie lacks the patience and willingness to understand her in-laws' culture without the help of her husband.

The issue of barrenness and the importance of children, themes in the Aidoo play, clearly exhibit two distinct sets of values and upbringings. In the contemporary urban Afro-American framework from which Eulalie comes, conjugality is the primary role of a married couple, while parenting is seen as an extension. Stress is placed upon an individual-oriented marriage. In the West African concept of marriage, parenting is dominant and is seen as the supreme expression of conjugality. In other words, the African marriage is primarily child-centred and family-oriented. This difference from the more individualized American setting explains the Yawson family's reaction on learning that Eulalie is not pregnant after a year of marriage. Ato's failure to explain to his family that he and Eulalie are practising birth control merely contributes to intensifying his family's bewilderment and disappointment.

Eulalie and Ato recognize reluctantly that their inherent value systems are being challenged. As a result, they experience alternately a sense of disbelief, indignation and hopelessness. Eulalie swears, smokes cigarettes, drinks heavily, and is openly contemptuous of her in-laws. In Act 5, Eulalie asks Ato:

> EU: Do you compare these bastards, these stupid narrow-minded savages with us? Do you dare?[4]

This outward behavior of Eulalie is contrary to her actual deep-seated needs. Her constant reliance on cigarettes, and alcoholic beverages[5] is an outward scream for attention, for she does want to belong to Ato's people:

> EU: . . . Ato, can't your Ma be sort of my Ma too?
> ATO: [*slowly and uncertainly*] Sure she can.
> EU: And your Pa mine?
> ATO: Sure.
>   [following lines solemn, like a prayer]
>   And all my people your people . . .

Though educated, Ato lacks the strength and drive to bridge the gap between Eulalie and his family, but his uneducated mother possesses the will to do so. At the end of the play it becomes evident that she will bring the couple together.

In both the Hansberry and Aidoo plays, the characters lack the maturity and insight necessary for the success of an intercultural marriage. The heroines of both plays, Beneatha and Eulalie respectively, are dreamers who are not attuned to the pressures they face. Asagai and Ato, the heroes, are consciously aware of the perils of intercultural marriages. Asagai can articulate them, but Ato finds it impossible.

Eulalie and Ato fail to agree on compromises and stipulations before marriage. Neither attempts to be more objective or tolerant. Furthermore, some of their problems might have been solved if they had travelled to Ghana before their marriage. Beneatha and Asagai appear to be somewhat more level-headed and will probably discuss the pros and cons of such a marriage, should a marriage, in fact, take place.

In *The Dilemma of a Ghost* one can speculate that the young Ama Ata Aidoo does not look kindly upon marriages between Afro-Americans and Ghanaians, because the play was written at the height of such marriages in Ghana. The most eligible, educated Ghanaian men were returning home after several years of education abroad with Afro-American, West Indian, and European wives. Most likely, Ama Ata Aidoo and other young, educated Ghanaian women resented this influx of foreign women, and those men who married outside of their ethnic groups. This reaction can explain why Eulalie is depicted as being crude, rootless, rude, insensitive and naive, and the characterization of Ato is no better. From the point of view of communication, Ato mumbles along, is unassertive and hesitant about decision-making, while Eulalie is bossy, aggressive and speaks in an unusually jazzy language which is not indigenous to Afro-Americans. For example, in Act 5, Ato talks to Eulalie about her drinking problem and Eulalie responds as follows:

EU: Poor darling Moses. Sure I have been drinking and on a Sunday morning: How dreadful? But surely Moses, it ain't matters on which God's day a girl gets soaked, eh?

EU: . . . Or are you too British you canna hear me Yankee lingo? (p. 85)

At the same time, Eulalie is a pathetic creature who needs to be treated firmly. What is so unbelievable about her characterization is her lack of tolerance and openmindedness, essential for a marriage, particularly an intercultural one. No woman in her right mind would marry a Ghanaian and openly call him 'Native Boy', and label his customs 'savage' as Eulalie does. One can only ask: Is Ms Aidoo saying that this is expected behaviour of a descendant of slaves who has married outside of her class? Is Ms Aidoo implying that an educated Afro-American woman is no great prize for an educated Ghanaian who can trace his family tree? Or perhaps the 20-year old Ms Aidoo was clairvoyant enough to see that a marriage between an Afro-American and Ghanaian is not easy and requires a definite strength of character and commitment from both partners.

It is safe to say that Ama Ata Aidoo attempts to look at intercultural marriages from a realistic point of view, despite the unbelievable behaviour of her two main characters. Her counterpart Lorraine Hansberry, on the other hand, maintains a romanticized vision of the possibility of such marriages. One assumes that Asagai wants to marry Beneatha (according to Harold Issacs)[6] in order to complete the passage from his traditional culture to the new world of modernism and change, for he leaves Beneatha with the statement: 'As-so this is what the new world hath finally wrought . . .' (p. 117). As for Beneatha, her concept of Africa is based upon illusions and preconceived notions of what she thinks Africa will be like. At times her ideas about Africa are blown out of proportion, and Asagai does not help to bring her back to reality.

In his autobiographical book, *The Rise and Fall of a Proper Negro*, Leslie Lacy observes the Afro-Americans who flocked to Ghana in the early 1960s in search of their dream world and identities. They:

> . . . soon discovered that our Africa was an illusion, and tried to relate to and love what they saw. The psychologically weak could not make this adjustment; even if he discovers the 'real Africa,' he is unable to embrace it, since it is not the Africa he wants. He would be criticizing himself. And given his understandable insecurities, he is unable and unwilling to do this . . . In short, he cannot dig Africa for what she is – changing, developing, confused, corrupt, beautiful, uncertain, flirting with revolution.[7]

Although Lacy's statement is not in direct reference to the Afro-American–West African marriage question, it aptly sums up the future of such marriages, if the two people involved cannot accept the real Africa, be willing to make the best of it and compromise, come to terms with their own inadequacies, and possess a self-confidence in *who* and *what* they are.

NOTES

1. Lorraine Hansberry, *A Raisin in the Sun*, New York, Signet, 1959, p. 67. All subsequent references are to this edition and appear in the text.
2. In his speech delivered at Howard University for the conference on 'The African Diaspora from a Changing Global Perspective' in August 1979, Julian Mayfield has called those blacks who believe there is a self-respecting status for them to win in the American society 'the last defenders of the American dream' or 'diehard integrationists'.
3. In an interview with Harold Issacs, Lorraine Hansberry said that she believed herself to be a 'strong nationalist' who also believed that 'all people and cultures must eventually merge into a common humanity . . .' The latter part of the statement clearly demonstrates Hansberry's misunderstanding of what constitutes a 'black nationalist'. See Harold R. Issacs, *The New World of American Negroes*, New York, Viking Press, 1963, p. 282.
4. Ama Ata Aidoo, *The Dilemma of a Ghost*, New York, Doubleday, 1971, pp. 86–7. All subsequent references are to this edition and appear in the text.
5. In a letter to the author dated 17 October 1980, Julian Mayfield remarked: 'Hardly any Afro woman in Ghana at the time Ama writes about could remotely be described as a street woman. Most were highly educated. Indeed, that was one of the reasons the Ghanaian men had been attracted to them.'
6. Issacs, *New World of American Negroes*, p. 299.
7. Leslie Lacy, *The Rise and Fall of the Proper Negro*, New York, Macmillan, 1971, p. 240.

Index